You Can Be Free

An Easy-to-Read Handbook for Abused Women

by Ginny NiCarthy and Sue Davidson

based on the book Getting Free:
You Can End Abuse and
Take Back Your Life
by Ginny NiCarthy

Seal Press

To Ruth L. Crow
in friendship, and in recognition of her enlightened work
for the rights and welfare of girls and women

© 1989, 1997 by Ginny NiCarthy and Sue Davidson

All rights reserved. No part of this book may be reproduced in any form, except for the quotation of brief passages in reviews, without prior permission from Seal Press, 3131 Western Avenue, Suite 410, Seattle, Washington 98121. Email: sealprss@scn.org.

Cover design by Patrick Barber

Library of Congress Cataloging-in-Publication Data
NiCarthy, Ginny.
   You can be free.
   (New leaf series)
   Simplified version of: Getting free / Ginny NiCarthy.
c1986.
   1. Abused women—United States—Handbooks, manuals,
etc.   2. Abused wives—United States—Handbooks, manuals,
etc.   I. Davidson, Sue, 1925–   II. NiCarthy, Ginny.
Getting free.   III. Title.
HV6626.N5 1989   362.8'3   88-36245
ISBN 1-878067-06-0

Printed in the United States of America
10   9

Distributed to the trade by Publishers Group West
In Canada: Publishers Group West Canada, Toronto
In Europe and the U.K.: Airlift Book Company, London
In Australia: Banyan Tree Book Distributors, Kent Town

Table of Contents

Acknowledgements

The first draft of this book was read by a number of Seattle reading experts who gave us a valuable critical comment. They are Sandra McNeill, Goodwill Literacy Adult Reading Center; Ann Muenchow, Marshall Alternative High School/Medina Children's Service; Laurie Cohen, Seattle Community College; Carol Essick and Linda R. Harris, Youth Employment Education Program. We made revisions of the manuscript on the basis of their written comments. Sandra McNeill and Ann Muenchow then asked a number of their students to read and evaluate sample chapters of the revised manuscript, and arranged for us to meet and talk with the students. In both content and form, the book benefitted greatly by the advice given us by this second set of readers. They are Tessa Bellows, Bernice Berry, Christina Blair, Roianne Bobo, Keva Bundy, Deborah Cole, Toosdy Fulsom, Serena Quinn and Stephanie Wood. Renè Lewis, teacher, participated helpfully in our discussion session at Goodwill. Our warm thanks are due to all these women.

We are also grateful for the good humor, solid support, and outstanding professional talents of our Seal Press editor, Faith Conlon.

Introduction

If you are being hurt by an intimate partner, you may be wondering how you got into this fix. You may be asking yourself if there is a way out. Perhaps you are thinking that your life is nothing like what you hoped for—and neither are you. Maybe you wish you could get back to the person you used to be.

You Can Be Free can help you build a more satisfying, safer life. Right now, you may be afraid of being struck or beaten. You probably feel humiliated or depressed a lot of the time. Sometimes you may feel very angry. These feelings can drain you of most of your energy. All this makes it hard to think clearly, much less to plan a way out. Reading this book can give you some breathing space, help you sort through your emotions and needs, and give you some tools for making changes.

You may have tried to change things in the past, or perhaps the person who abuses you promised to stop. But then it happened again. Maybe your partner says it is your fault. You worry that this may be so. But if someone mistreats you, it is that person's responsibility to change. If your partner has hurt you many times, you may have called the police or asked family members for help. Perhaps they didn't believe you or said you brought the abuse on yourself. Or they asked: "Why don't you just leave?"

It has been hard for people to understand why it is so difficult to leave an abusive partner. But there is much more understanding of such problems today, thanks to the movement against domestic violence. Over the past twenty years laws have been changed to offer protection to women who are abused. As recently as 1994 the United States Congress has recognized the problem by providing money for a national hotline twenty-four hours a day, ready to help you, no matter where you are or who you are.

Perhaps you live in a rural area, or do not speak English, or you are deaf, or disabled, or a member of a minority group. Hotline workers will help you find women to talk to; who can speak your language; or who are part of your community. They will listen; give you information about how to be safe; help you make a plan. If you have children, it is urgent that you work out plans to protect them from bodily harm.

The hotline number is 1-800-799-7233.

You might decide to leave an abusive partner. If so, it is very important to make a safety plan. If your partner has struck you or threatened to, the violence is likely to get worse when you say you are going to leave. Your partner might do everything possible to track you down. So you will probably need to make plans to be in a place where he—or she—cannot find and hurt you further.

Throughout this book you will find stories of women who were abused. These women—women like you—describe ways they handled the same problems you are facing. They tell about how they have changed their lives. They describe what it is like, at last, to feel safe and to feel that their children are safe. Through this book, they speak to you. Like them, you too can be free.

Ginny NiCarthy and Sue Davidson
Seattle
May 1997

Chapter 1

What is Abuse?

"It got worse each time he hit me. Afterwards he would drive off or go to work and the next day he'd be sorry. I was ready to make up, because I was so scared. I didn't have any place to go, I didn't want to live with my parents, and I was scared to be out in the cold."

— Lynn

When you are hurt by a person you love, you feel alone. You think, "Other women don't have this problem." But many women are hurt by their partners. The partner might be a boyfriend the woman lives with. Or it could be her husband or her lover.

- Between 20 and 50 percent of women are hit by partners at least once.
- Many more women suffer from emotional abuse.

Maybe you're still not sure this describes your problem. "Emotional abuse." "Battering." "Wife-beating." You've heard all those terms before. But what do they mean, exactly? Do they mean the same things? Are they all different?

ABUSE

Abuse means mistreating another person. Abuse may be physical, emotional, or sexual. The word "abuse" can be used to mean each of these things. Or it can be used to mean all three of them.

1

BATTERING (PHYSICAL ABUSE)

Battering is physical abuse. "Wife-beating" is another name people sometimes use for battering. But many women who are battered are not wives.

Battering is not just one hit. It's a *pattern* of physical assaults, threats, or restraints. It is violence used to control another person. Men who batter scare women into doing what they want them to do.

Has your partner done any of these things:

- Slapped, pushed, shoved, bit? Hit with a fist?
- Blocked you from leaving a room or a house?
- Thrown things or destroyed property?
- Hit walls or pounded his fist when angry?
- Kicked, burned, choked, beaten, or raped you?
- Used a gun, knife, or other weapon against you, or threatened to use one?

Have any of these things happened:

- Have you had to stay in bed or been too weak to work, after being hit?
- Have you had bruises from being hit, held, or squeezed?
- Have you had a black eye, cut lip, or broken tooth from being attacked?
- Have you ever seen a doctor as a result of injuries from your partner?
- Has your partner ever kept you from seeing a doctor when you needed to?
- Have you ever been hospitalized as a result of your partner's violence?

If your answer to any of these questions is yes, you have been physically abused. If it has happened more than once, you are probably being battered.

Sometimes women abuse men. They even hit men. But they hardly ever batter men. Men are usually not afraid of being hurt by women. So it is hard for a woman to control a man by force. And battering is a *pattern of control.*

A person who batters almost always uses emotional abuse, too.

EMOTIONAL ABUSE

Emotional abuse is mistreating and controlling another person through her feelings. It includes insulting, giving orders, and saying things to confuse the partner. The emotional abuser makes the partner feel afraid, helpless, or worthless. Has your partner done these things:

- Ignored you, called you names, made fun of you?
- Controlled the money, car, decisions?
- Threatened to leave you regularly?
- Told you about his affairs with other women?
- Punished the children when he was angry at you?
- Abused pets to hurt you?

If so, you are emotionally abused. There are many, many ways that a person can be abused emotionally. Chapter 2 will tell you a lot more about emotional abuse.

SEXUAL ABUSE

Sexual abuse is mistreatment by means of sexual acts, demands, or insults. It can be partly physical and partly emotional. Or it can be just one or the other. Has your partner done these things:

- Called you sexual names, like "frigid," "whore"?
- Scared you so much you had sex when you didn't want to?
- Made you have sex when it was painful or you were sick?

- Not told you he had V.D.?
- Not let you use birth control?
- Refused to use a condom to protect you from V.D. or AIDS?

If these things have been done to you, you are sexually abused.

Now turn to Chapter 2, to learn more about emotional abuse.

Chapter 2

Emotional Abuse

Does your partner often make you feel bad even without hitting you? Do you wonder whether it's your fault that he doesn't treat you better? If so, this chapter may help you see things more clearly.

The questions below will help you know what is being done to you. Check each one with the answer that fits: either "often," "sometimes," or "never."

Activity 1   Emotional Abuse Checklist

Keeping You Away from Other People

	Often	Sometimes	Never
1. Does your partner get angry when you talk on the phone?	_____	_____	_____
2. Does he open your mail?	_____	_____	_____
3. Does he keep you from seeing friends?	_____	_____	_____
4. Is he angry when you are just a little late getting home?	_____	_____	_____
5. Does he want you home when he is home?	_____	_____	_____

	Often	Sometimes	Never

Always on Your Mind

6. *Do you worry about what he will think of your make-up? Or how you dress?* _____ _____ _____

7. *Do you ask him who you can see or where you can go?* _____ _____ _____

8. *Are you careful of what you say, so that he won't get upset?* _____ _____ _____

9. *Do you feel that you're "walking on eggshells"?* _____ _____ _____

Putting You Down; Humiliation

10. *Does he call you names, like "stupid," "bitch," "cunt"?* _____ _____ _____

11. *Does he tell you what is "wrong" with you in front of other people?* _____ _____ _____

12. *Has he made you do things that make you feel ashamed?* _____ _____ _____

13. *Does he say no one else would want you?* _____ _____ _____

Threats

14. *Does he threaten to leave you?* _____ _____ _____

15. *Has he said he will go crazy or kill himself if you leave?* _____ _____ _____

16. *Has he refused to "let" you go out, unless you do as he says?* _____ _____ _____

	Often	Sometimes	Never
17. Does he say he will hit you or beat you if you don't obey?	_____	_____	_____

Feeling Sick and Tired

	Often	Sometimes	Never
18. Does he keep you up late, asking about men in your past?	_____	_____	_____
19. Do you work so hard to please him that you feel worn out?	_____	_____	_____
20. Do you feel sick, yet you're not sure what's wrong?	_____	_____	_____
21. Are you unable to do things you used to do easily?	_____	_____	_____

Small Demands

	Often	Sometimes	Never
22. Does he demand that dinner be served right on the minute?	_____	_____	_____
23. Does he insist that the house look just so?	_____	_____	_____
24. Do you have to report how you spend every dollar?	_____	_____	_____

Sweet-Talk and Treats

	Often	Sometimes	Never
25. After he has been mean, does he act sweet and loving?	_____	_____	_____
26. After he has hit you, does he give you a present or take you out?	_____	_____	_____
27. When you decide to leave, does he give you hope for change?	_____	_____	_____

There is no "right" or "wrong" score. But see how many checks you put under "sometimes" or "often." If you checked many, there is a pattern of control. Everyone tries to control another person once in a while. But a *pattern* of controlling a person through feelings is emotional abuse.

The pattern will show up in many ways. Your partner wants you to obey him. He acts as if you can't make decisions on your own. He treats you like a small child who can't be trusted.

When you want to leave, he threatens you. Or he acts sweet, so you will stay. He acts nice to you sometimes—just enough to give you hope.

Notice the headings for the methods of control. They are at the beginning of each set of questions, above. Prison guards use methods like these to make prisoners of war obey. These methods are called "brainwashing."

Why is brainwashing used against prisoners? Because you can't completely control people even when they are in a prison. Fences and guards are not enough to control them. The best way to control people is through their minds.

There are many ways to control people's minds. One way is to scare them into thinking they have no power. Another is to make people believe they are worthless. When they feel scared, helpless, and worthless, they won't try to make changes. If that is how you feel, your partner might be causing it. He may be brainwashing you.

Many women are shocked to learn that men do this. You might be wondering if your partner is doing it on purpose. He might not want to admit that he is brainwashing you. He might say he is only doing it because he loves you.

There are two more kinds of emotional abuse that are common.

1. *"Crazy-making."* Is your partner telling you one thing today and another the next day? Lying about things that are not at all important? Saying you are crazy, or you imagine things? If he does these things often, you might begin to feel confused. You might even think you *are* going crazy.

2. *Ignoring you and neglecting you.* Is your partner not paying attention when you talk to him? Not caring about your feelings? Not telling you how he feels? Refusing to give you money you need for food? Or for the children?

Acting that way is also emotional abuse. If he doesn't hear you and doesn't see you, you might feel invisible. That makes it hard to feel that you are worth much.

Maybe you emotionally abuse your partner. If so, that is a serious problem, too. But it doesn't change what he is doing to you.

Many women say that emotional abuse is worse than physical. But physical abuse can kill you or do permanent damage. Physical violence also causes a lot of fear. Together, emotional and physical abuse have a powerful effect.

Melissa, a white woman, had been abused as a child. She was doing well in college when she fell in love with Tom. When they started living together, he insisted that she leave college. Tom's abuse started slowly, then got worse and worse.

"He had me believing that I was fat, that I was a bitch, a whore. I felt like a prisoner... not human. If I were beaten, so what? I would have been too embarrassed to discuss what was happening with my friends, and I was totally isolated from them anyway."

Lisa is a Tlingit Indian, abused by two husbands, both of them white. Telling about the second husband, she said:

"He would try to make love after he beat me.... After he beat me, he bought me things all the time.... I couldn't relate to anyone, couldn't explain how I could be locked into one little corner of my mind and not remember anything. It was like going crazy....

"He moved out and we started making new lives, but he was at every one of the softball games I played in, just watching, making me nervous. Then he started... bringing me flowers."

Lisa and Melissa both got away from their abusive partners. Melissa has begun to take up the activities she left when she met Tom. Lisa has a good job working for the state of Alaska. She is married now to a man who treats her well.

Chapter 3

Why Does Abuse Go On?

Now you have read about different kinds of abuse. You may have decided that you are being abused by your partner. If so, this book can help you. It can help you decide whether to stay with the man, or leave. It can help you solve new problems you will face if you leave. Each chapter can help you build a safer, better life.

But you are only one woman among many. Millions of women are abused every day. You may ask: How can this go on? Why does it happen? Can anything be done to stop it?

This chapter will give you some answers to those questions. It will help you see that changes are possible.

BACKGROUND OF THE PROBLEM

Until recently, many people thought men had a right to batter their women. Wife-beating was even protected by law. Then, in some countries, the laws began to change. In the United States, wife-beating became illegal early in this century.

But battering still went on, even though it wasn't legal. Most people thought it was a private matter. They didn't think society ought to meddle in it. It wasn't discussed in public. Nobody wrote about it in the newspapers. It was kept hidden.

Today, there are still people who want to keep battering hidden. They pretend it doesn't happen. Or it's not serious. Or the woman brought it on herself. Friends and relatives may refuse to see the problem. Doctors, lawyers, police, and judges also may ignore it. Is it any wonder the battered woman feels alone?

Jennifer remembers what it was like, feeling there was nobody she could talk to. People acted as if there was something wrong with *her*, not the batterer! She says:

"I needed somebody to say, 'It's not your fault. You're not making him be this way and you can't make him *not* be this way.' Nobody was saying that. One friend's response was, 'Well, that's not really battering. It's not *that* serious. You didn't break any bones.'"

ATTITUDES ARE CHANGING

During the 1970s, women began to speak up about battering. They gave support to women who chose to leave violent men. They helped women who wanted to prosecute the men who battered them.

They insisted that the public listen. More people began to admit that battering happened. More people began to see that battering wasn't just a private problem. They began to see that it was society's problem, too.

Now it has become possible to do some of these things:

- make laws to protect women who are abused
- educate doctors, nurses, and counselors about abuse
- educate police, lawyers, prosecutors, and judges about abuse

Now more people are asking these questions:

- Why does he batter?

• Why does he stay?
• Why does she stay?

THE MALE IMAGE

Our society tells men they should be like this:

• self-confident
• forceful
• able to control and hide emotion
• active
• fearless

• physically tough
• good at sports
• adventurous
• wise to the ways of the world
• sexually powerful

Imagine trying to live up to all that! Very few men can. When they try to, they often fail. Some men feel weak and inferior when they fail. To save face, they may lash out, blaming whoever is handy. That is one way to hide their painful feelings.

WHY DO MEN BATTER?

Love may make a man feel dependent and weak. It may make him feel that his partner has power over him.

Many of us resent those who have power over us. For men, it's worse. They think they're not supposed to feel powerless and weak. They may get especially upset if a woman makes them feel weak. They think they're supposed to be superior to women. If they can't feel that way, they may become very angry.

The more a man cares about his strong male image, the more angry he may become. His anger will be directed at the one who makes him feel weak. In other words, at the one he loves.

Anger Doesn't Explain Battering

People who live together may get angry for a lot of reasons. Most couples have disagreements. They may argue over money, chores, or the children. These arguments sometimes lead to anger.

But anger does not explain why a man batters a woman. Most of the time, people who are angry do not hit anybody.

What about a Violent Childhood?

About 60 percent of violent men were beaten as children. Or they saw one parent batter another. But this does not completely explain battering, either. What about the other 40 percent? Some men from abusive families never hit anybody.

No Simple Answer

So why would a man batter a woman he loves? There is no simple answer to this question. Instead, there seem to be a lot of answers. Here are some of them:

- He wants to control her.
- He's afraid he's weak, so he acts tough.
- He knows she won't tell.
- He doesn't think he'll be punished, if she does tell.
- Society has not taught him that battering is a crime.
- His father battered his mother, so it doesn't seem wrong.
- His parents battered him, so it doesn't seem wrong.

WHY DO MEN STAY?

The man who batters may be very dependent on the woman. A violent man often has a hard time forming relationships. His female partner may be the only person he feels close to.

The abuser won't leave, because he feels his woman is all he has. He may be very afraid of losing her. That makes him jealous. He thinks she wants other men. He hopes that by beating her, he can scare her into being faithful. At least, he can frighten her so much that she won't dare leave him.

THE FEMALE IMAGE

Society expects women to be like this:

- very emotional
- fearful
- passive
- home-bound
- physically weaker than men
- easily led by others
- dependent
- lacking in self-confidence
- very interested in clothing, hair styles, make-up

Most of these ideas of women are untrue as well as harmful. Yet women are portrayed this way in school books, magazine ads, and on TV. Parents and teachers back up these ideas. So does religion.

Most parents want girls to be sweet, quiet, and pretty. In school books, girls are pictured as timid. They stand around watching boys being "naughty" or brave. They hardly ever have adventures of their own.

TV and magazine ads show adult women trying to please men. In the ads, women work hard at being beautiful. They curl their hair and paint their faces. They seem to spend their lives mainly at home.

Most religions teach that women should be meek. They teach that women should serve others and should obey men.

What does this all add up to? It adds up to the idea that women are weak and helpless. Also, that they aren't very smart.

How could it be good for anybody to be weak, helpless,

and stupid? Yet, in general, society tells women that's the way they should be. They are told that they aren't strong enough to take care of themselves. They are taught that they need a strong man to protect them.

WHY DO WOMEN STAY?

In spite of what society tells them, many women do take care of themselves. They know how to deal with the world. They are independent. They make their own decisions. They feel they're strong.

It might seem that a strong, independent woman couldn't be abused. It might seem that a woman must be weak and helpless to be abused. But that is not so.

Society tells every woman that to be a "whole person" she must have a male partner. So a woman who has a man often does not want to lose him. What if she never gets another one?

It is not only weak or helpless women who have such fears. A strong, capable woman may put up with a lot to keep the man she loves.

A woman might stay with an abuser for other reasons, too. Here are some of them:

Fear of Poverty

Most women earn lower pay than their husbands. Some women don't earn enough to support themselves and their children. They're afraid to leave a man, even though he batters. They are afraid of being poor.

Other women are able to work at good jobs. But they may still have money troubles after a divorce or separation. After divorce, a woman's income is almost always reduced. Most divorced women take the main responsibility for children. They have more things to pay for, and less money to spend. Many women are afraid to take this risk.

Fear of the Abuser

The man who batters may threaten to kill the woman if she leaves. Or he may say he'll kill her parents or her children. He says he will track her down wherever she goes. Perhaps he has done it before when she left. She's afraid she will be in even more danger if she leaves.

Other Reasons

A woman's ethnic, religious, or family group may not accept divorce or separation. She's afraid her group will reject her if she leaves her husband. That might make her stay with him.

A woman may also stay because she doesn't want to break up the family. She may believe the children should have a father. Or she may love the abuser and feel guilty and worried about him.

There are many reasons an abused woman stays. The next chapters will look at these reasons more closely.

WHAT CAN BE DONE?

Today, more and more women are saying "No!" to battering. They are changing laws. They are changing people's ideas. They have created new services, such as shelters for battered women.

There is a lot more to be done. But it is easier now for a battered woman to get help than at any other time in history.

With the help of each other, women are finding ways to free themselves from violence. Usually, they must do this by separating from an abusive man. Deciding whether to leave or stay is the first hard step to being free.

Chapter 4

Is It Ever Right to Break Up the Family?

Maybe you've decided what you *want* to do. You want to leave the man who abuses you. But you're not sure it's what you *should* do. You may have thoughts like these:

"A woman's place is with her man."

"A woman doesn't leave just because of a few family fights."

"You can't run away from your problems."

"The family should stay together through thick and thin and work things out."

WHOSE IDEAS?

Where do those thoughts come from? Are they your ideas, or someone else's? Are they what your mother says? Your husband? Your minister? Your counselor? Your father?

Once you know where the ideas come from, you can decide whether you agree. Do you really believe these things? Or do you just say them to yourself without thinking about what they mean? Do you think a wife should stick by her husband, no matter how he treats her?

You may decide that it's wrong to put up with an abusive man. But you're still not sure you should leave. You worry a lot over thoughts like these:

"He'll fall apart."

18

"He has nothing else."
"He'll kill himself."
"I can't deprive him of the kids."

WILL HE REALLY FALL APART?

People do "crack up." They do kill themselves. What are the chances that your worst fears may come true? No one can say for sure. But some questions may help sort things out.

Has he "cracked up" before? Has he tried suicide or had a mental breakdown in the past? If he had mental problems before you met, you're not the cause of them.

He may crack up again if you leave. But he may not. He may be able to handle stress better now than in the past. It isn't true that everything he does depends on you.

Has he talked about suicide? There is a common belief that people who talk about suicide don't do it. This is not true.

You can't really be sure what he'll do. But that doesn't mean you have to stay with him. And there may be ways you can help him. Just remember that your first job is to help yourself.

How Can You Help?

If you decide to leave, you might find someone to stay with him. His friends or family members might help. They have to be people he's willing to be with.

He can also seek the help of a counselor. You can suggest that he go to counseling. But that's all you can do. The rest is up to him.

Remember, there is a limit to what you can do to help him. Sooner or later, he has to help himself. He has to stop leaning on you. If he won't, then you're right back where you started.

WHAT ABOUT THE CHILDREN?

Suppose that you have decided to leave. You have decided to take the children. He may be very angry or hurt. He may say that it's the end of his relationship with them. That you'll turn them against him. That they'll grow away from him.

That might make you feel too guilty to leave. But there's no reason to accept the picture he's drawn. A father and his children can be close without living in the same house. Their relationship will depend a lot upon how he acts.

Some fathers normally spend little time with their children. They may see them for a few minutes before bedtime. They might spend half a weekend day with them. A father may actually spend more time with his children after a separation. He may have to care for them for twenty-four hours, for the first time. When he takes care of their daily needs, he may feel closer to them.

However, you may decide you must cut all ties. You may need to disappear so that the man can't find you. This would be the case if he is a threat to your life. Or a threat to your children's lives.

Fathers sometimes threaten to kidnap children. Usually, it's an empty threat. But it does happen. If you think it really might happen, you need legal advice. You may also want to see a counselor, to cope with your anxiety.

CHILD ABUSE

Are your children battered, as well as you? Many adults think it's all right to hit children to punish them. They may not know child abuse when they see it.

Child abuse is punishment that has gotten out of control. It's punishment that puts cuts, welts, burns, or bruises on a child. It can result in lifelong damage, or death. A child needs to be kept safely away from an abuser. Children don't have the power to protect themselves.

If your children are abused, you can take steps to protect them. The best way is to leave the abuser and take the children with you.

You may fear that your abusive husband will get custody if you separate. But there are some ways you can guard against that. Let other people know that he abuses the children. Be sure you take the children to a doctor when their father hurts them. Do this whether or not they need treatment. Ask the doctor to record the injuries. You'll be able to use the record later if there's a custody dispute.

Are you the one who's violent to the children? The first step in solving the problem is to admit it. The second step is asking for help. This may be hard to do. But you'll be relieved once your secret is out. People who understand your problem are there to give you practical help. You will learn better ways to discipline and enjoy your children. Look in the telephone book for these helpful people:

- Parents Anonymous
- a counselor or crisis line
- state health/welfare services, children's protective division

Sexual Abuse of Children

Incest is the sexual abuse of children by family members. It happens in families of all classes and races. Batterers are not the only people who abuse children sexually. But batterers often do. The victims may be the woman's children, or both his and hers.

Don't depend on the child to tell you. The abuser has probably made threats about what he'll do if she tells. (Or if he tells—boys are abused, too.)

If you have any suspicions, don't wait. Find a quiet

place to be with the child alone. Bring up the topic. Explain that you won't blame the child for whatever has happened.

Some adults claim that a child can provoke incest by "sexy" behavior. This is a way of shifting blame to the child. But it's adults who have power over children—not the other way around. It's the adult who is responsible for the abuse.

WHAT DO THE CHILDREN DESERVE?

What positive things do the children gain from their father? Love? Security? Affection? Respect? Money? Stability? Fun?

Don't assume they'll lose all these if they're not living with him. They may just get them in different ways, at different times. Custody plans can allow for an ongoing relationship.

There may be less money for the children. This can be hard for them. But is it as hard for them as living with a man who batters? Do they deserve the right to be free of fear? The right to be free of humiliation?

Perhaps the father does not bully and insult the children. This emotional abuse may be confined to you. But the children see his brutal treatment of you. They might grow up thinking that's the way adults treat each other. Would you like them to learn something different?

If you stay, you set an example. The child sees an adult who is helpless in the face of violence. The message is: "When people you love hit you, you just have to take it."

Janine, a Latina, talked about the effects of her separation on her daughter:

"When Raul and I were still together, she had ear infections, she was fussy, she wouldn't sleep... something

was always wrong. Once he left she gained weight, she grew, she just really changed. She's happy. She shines. A big weight was lifted off of her and she was allowed to grow. That's the big thing that made me not want to go back to him. I didn't think I had the right to take her peace of mind away."

Many people believe that children are better off in two-parent homes. In fact, there is no evidence that they are. It depends upon what kind of home it is. There *is* some evidence that males who have violent fathers may become violent adults.

Female children are influenced, as well. They may accept battering as normal behavior for a mate. In their turn, they may become victims as adults.

Your children deserve as safe a home as you can provide. They deserve a home where people respect each other. They deserve a chance to grow into healthy adults.

Chapter 5

What Do You Owe Yourself?

The person who abuses you acts as if you had no rights. So you're probably afraid to act as if you do. By now, you may not even feel that you have any rights. But you do. This chapter will help you to realize what they are.

ARE YOU SOMEBODY BESIDES WIFE, MOTHER, OR GIRLFRIEND?

Many women can't tell where the family leaves off and they begin. They feel they're just a part of their children or their husbands. They forget that they have a separate identity.

Try to answer these questions:

1. What do I want?
2. What do I want to do now?
3. What do I like to do?
4. Whom do I like to spend time with?
5. What do I like to wear?
6. Where do I like to go?
7. Where would I like to live?
8. What do I want to be doing in five years?
9. What do I want to be doing in ten years? Twenty years?

How many of your answers were something like this:

24

"I want to live here because moving would mean changing the kids' schools."

"He likes me to wear. . . . "

"I don't much care—I'm easy to please."

"My husband wouldn't hear of it."

"It costs too much."

If your answers were like that, they don't say what you want. They are about what other people want. Or they say what you think can't happen, rather than what you want.

Try answering again. This time, don't think about how other family members would be affected. This doesn't mean you don't care about them. It simply means that you deserve some things you want. It means that you count for something. You are a person, too.

After she left, Maddie began to see herself as someone important:

"I could almost say I was born again. When I was with him, all I thought about was him and the kids. But when we were separated, I was in tip-top shape. I felt up!"

MIND-READING

Women are taught to think of the needs of others. It's supposed to be part of their role—especially as wives and mothers.

Young children can't say how they feel or what they need. Their caretakers—mostly women—have to figure out their needs for them. But adult men are able to say what they need or want. Why don't they do it? Why does a woman have to guess what a man is feeling?

It is partly because men are taught not to express emotion. That's why a man may depend on his woman to guess what he's feeling. Is he depressed? Frightened? Lonely?

Does he want comfort? Even if he hasn't asked her, the woman is supposed to give it.

An abused woman tries hard to read the abuser's mind. Her health and safety may depend on it. If she's not tuned in to what her partner wants, he may explode.

However, some violent men explode even if their needs *are* met. You need to notice how far mind-reading goes in making you safe. You also need to ask yourself if it's worth the strain. Are you willing to go on walking on eggshells forever? Do you owe yourself a chance at something better?

WHAT IF IT'S REALLY MY FAULT?

"Maybe I brought it on myself."
"I started it last time, by nagging him."
"I'm a sloppy housekeeper."
"I'm cold in bed."
"Sometimes I hit him back."
"He puts up with a lot from me."

You're aware that you have faults, too. This makes you feel that you're responsible for the abuse. It may keep you from thinking of ending the relationship. Instead, you think: "If only I can change, he'll change too."

But what changes will really keep him from hitting you? Make a list of things you did that he says "caused" him to hit you. Maybe the house wasn't perfectly clean. Or dinner was late. Or you spent time with women friends. Did you get hit every time you did those things? *Only* then? Were you hit sometimes for no reason at all?

Which of your "faults" do you want to correct? Do any of them give him the right to "discipline" you with a beating? Let's take as an example your spending time with women friends.

Do you deserve to have friends? Friends can give you

what you don't get from him. Friends will talk to you and listen to you. They show they care about you and like you. Every person deserves these things.

You may try to get along without the comfort you get from friends. But then you get lonely and depressed. So you take a chance and secretly meet your friend. If he finds out and beats you, does that mean you were wrong? Is it really a fault to want friends? Is it really something you want to change?

Does one adult have the right to punish another? No. This right would mean that the man has the authority to control you. And to use violence to do it. *He does not have either of those rights.* Whether or not you have faults is beside the point. You are not his property or his child. In fact, the law now limits the rights of parents to punish children.

WHAT ARE YOUR RIGHTS?

It's likely that you've given up your rights little by little. Perhaps you didn't even notice it was happening. Freedom of speech—a basic right—is usually the first to go. An abused woman stops talking about things that might upset her man. Here are some of the things you may have stopped talking about:

1. Past relationships. (He gets jealous.)
2. Dreams for the future. (He thinks you're complaining about how things are now.)
3. Questions about his work, what he's done, how he feels. (He accuses you of prying or nagging.)
4. Statements of your opinions. (He doesn't want to hear what you think. "You're stupid.")
5. Statements about feeling down—sad, lonely, or discouraged. (He doesn't want to hear your complaints.)

It may be hard for you to realize what your rights are. Here is a list of rights that everyone is entitled to.

LIST OF RIGHTS

1. The right to state opinions, including unpopular ones.
2. The right to express feelings, even if you feel down.
3. The right to privacy.
4. The right to choose religion and lifestyle.
5. The right to be free of fear.
6. The right to have some time for yourself.
7. The right to spend some money as you please.
8. The right to paid employment, at fair wages.
9. The right to choose your friends.
10. The right to emotional support from family and friends.
11. The right to be listened to by family and friends.
12. The right to decide whether to have sex or not.

Draw a line under each of the rights you think everyone deserves. Next, *circle* the rights that you have now. Is there a difference between your rights and those of others? Ask yourself whether that means that you aren't a person. Or does it mean that wives don't have rights? That women don't have rights? That mothers don't, until their children are grown?

For many women, it's hardest to believe they have rights to time and money. Let's look briefly at those two.

Money

Perhaps there's not enough money, even to pay basic bills. Still, some money is always spent on things you don't have to have. Does the grocery bag contain candy, pop, beer, cigarettes? If so, someone has already made some decisions about what is "needed."

It's hard to decide how family money should be spent. But *both* adults—not just the man—should decide. Compromises can be worked out. Each person should have something to spend, no questions asked. The amount may be small. But it's hers or his to spend.

If you're sneaking money, you're acting as if you don't have rights. You're acting like someone who isn't allowed to make her own decisions.

Time

Each of you should have some time to spend as you please. It should be at least one half-day, and one evening a week.

You may not know what to do with your time, at first. Take it, anyway. Go to a movie that your partner doesn't want to see. Walk in the park, take a class. Doing what *you* choose will help you begin to build your own identity.

GETTING RESPECT FOR YOUR WORK AT HOME OR FOR PAY

Some people still believe that the man should be the sole provider. They think of a woman's earnings as "a little extra." For most families, that's not true anymore. As living costs rise, most families need and use the woman's income.

Ideas about work have changed in recent years. More people have begun to accept the following ideas:

- Work is of equal value, whether done by a man or a woman.
- Women need adequate pay, just as men do.
- Both partners in a marriage should share house and child care.

• Work in the home is as important as work outside the home.

Suppose your partner wants you to stay at home. Yet he looks down on the work you do there. After a while, you might begin to agree. You feel the work isn't important and you're not important.

If that's what's happening, you need to change something. You may need to relearn respect for your work at home. List all the reasons you think it's important. If you still don't believe it, you may need to look for a paid job.

Maybe you already work outside the home. But neither you nor your partner think it's important. In that case, you may need to get training for a better job. In other words, start respecting what you do or doing what you respect.

CLAIMING YOUR RIGHTS

Look at the List of Rights on page 28. Decide which rights you want to begin claiming. Is it safe to discuss them with your partner? You could start with agreements about time and money. Will he keep to his part of the bargain?

If the answers are no, you owe it to yourself to consider leaving.

You have rights, like anyone else. But you have to believe in them, yourself. That's the first step in getting them.

Chapter 6

"But I Still Love Him"

There are three kinds of love between couples. These are:

- romantic love
- addictive love
- nurturing love

At times, the three overlap. But they can be looked at separately, too.

Which kind of love do you and your partner share? This exercise will help you to find out. *Put a check mark* in front of each of the following that seems true.

Activity 2   How Do You Love Each Other?

1. *I could never love anyone else the way I love him.*
2. *Without him, I have nothing to live for.*
3. *I know exactly what it is about him I love.*
4. *I suppose I should be interested in other people and activities. But I just want to be with him.*
5. *We help each other to explore new ideas.*
6. *Whenever I'm a few minutes late, he thinks I'm with another man.*
7. *I wear my "rose-colored glasses" and see only the best in him.*

8. *The thought of his being with anyone else makes me miserable.*
9. *I hope he never leaves me. But if it comes to that, I'll be okay.*
10. *He could never love another woman the way he loves me.*
11. *Often, I feel better when I'm away from him. But then I call him anyway.*
12. *I never let him see me without makeup or wearing curlers. I want him always to see me at my best.*
13. *He brings out the best in me.*
14. *I don't know why I love him, I just do.*
15. *He has many of the qualities I value. They are qualities I'm trying to develop in myself.*
16. *It's wonderful to spend time alone with him, and also together with others. I also enjoy being by myself and with women friends.*
17. *He's so special. I don't know why he's interested in an ordinary person like me.*
18. *Without me, he has nothing to live for.*
19. *He wants me to feel good whether I'm with him or not.*
20. *This time he means it. He's really going to change.*
21. *He wants to know where I am every minute. That's how I know he loves me.*
22. *I like to hear about the good times he has with other people.*

ROMANTIC LOVE

Romantic love is supposed to be magic. It's supposed to go like this: Two people meet. They know at once that they were made for each other. They weren't meant for anybody else in the world. There's nothing they can do about it. They are helpless in the face of their love.

These ideas are very popular. We hear songs about them. We read stories about them and see movies about them.

Look at your responses to 1, 7, 10, 12, 14, 17. The more you checked, the more romantic your ideas about love are. To keep them, you have to hide a lot from yourself. And from him.

You are deeply in love with the idea of your man. You don't want that idea to be shaken by his real behavior. Never mind the facts. He's wonderful. You're perfect for each other. He'll stop his cruelty soon. The magic of your love will go on and on.

ADDICTIVE LOVE

Romantic love can be experienced as a kind of "high." For some women, this is not dangerous. It's not dangerous for a woman who likes herself. It's not dangerous for one who values other friends and interests. If her man stops loving her, she'll mourn for a while. But her entire world won't fall to pieces.

But some women place a low value on themselves and their interests. Love overwhelms everything else in their lives. For such a woman, romantic love can cross over into addiction. Her world shrinks to nothing but her need for the man. She'll be certain she can't live without his love. She'll put up with anything from him, just to keep it.

Her life may become an addictive cycle. There is the "high" when her need for him is fulfilled. Then comes the "downer" when the "supply" is removed. She is completely dependent on getting her supply. She can't get it from anybody but him.

Sometimes the man, too, feels that he can't live without the woman. They are addicted *to each other*. Men who batter are even more dangerous when they are addicted to the woman. They may go to any lengths to keep a woman from leaving.

Did you check 6, 18, 21? These indicate that the man is

addicted to you. Did you check 2, 4, 8, 11, 20? Checks for these reflect your addiction to him.

Amanda says:
"I felt like a damned junkie trying to hide the tracks. I was a Sam junkie. I've been going through withdrawal ever since."

NURTURING LOVE

Nurturing love is the opposite of addictive love. It promotes growth and strength rather than dependence. It is based on real appreciation of the loved one's good traits. But neither partner has to pretend that the other has no flaws.

Nurturing love helps each partner to improve. It expands the world of each. It does not cut off other relationships and interests.

Look at your responses to 3, 5, 9, 13, 15, 16, 19, 22. The more of these you checked, the more nurturing your love is. The man in such a relationship may sometimes get angry at his partner. (So may the woman.) But he would not abuse his partner.

CAN YOU LEAVE SOMEONE YOU LOVE?

Loving an abusive man makes it hard to leave, but not impossible. The most loving thing may be to separate, even if it's temporary. Nobody wants their loved one to continue a round of violence. If the relationship is also an addictive one, your course is clear. You'll need to end it immediately and totally.

If you want to leave, you'll need to give up certain romantic ideas. These are ideas like: "He's the only one who can give me what I need." "I'll never find another man to love." "My life's not worth living if I don't have love all the time."

There was a time when Dee thought she couldn't live without Pete. Now she says:

"I can remember years and years of saying to myself, I love this man, how can I help him. . . . I would never go back to him, because I'm so happy now."

Chapter 7

Making the Decision to Leave or Stay

Some battered women read every word they can find on abuse. But the reading doesn't give them what they want. They hope to find a solution that doesn't require leaving the man. Or a solution that doesn't mean risk. Or one that won't bring pain.

There are no solutions like that. If you change your life, it will bring you rewards. It will be challenging. It may even be exciting. But it may also be hard, lonely, and frightening, at first.

Are you serious about making changes in your life? If so, it's time to face the facts, and then act. The facts may not be as awful as you think.

WHAT'S THE WORST THAT CAN HAPPEN
IF YOU LEAVE?

You may imagine terrible things happening: "I'll be so depressed, I'll take an overdose of pills." "I won't be able to support the children. Then I'll lose custody of them." Maybe your fears are less dramatic: "How will I discipline the children by myself?" "I'll be stuck at my office job forever. I'll never be able to get ahead."

Perhaps your worst fears are more vague: "Being alone." Try to make the frightening thought specific. Is it sex you'll miss when you're alone? Someone to go places with? Someone to lean on and be needed by?

36

Write down your worst fear of what might happen. Then *list* reasons it's likely to happen, and reasons it's unlikely. For example, your worst fear might be "losing the house." A reason it's likely might be "can't meet the payments." A reason it's unlikely might be "can rent out rooms if kids double up."

Activity 3   Worst Fears List

Worst Fear: _____

Reasons It's Likely	*Reasons It's Unlikely*
_____	_____
_____	_____
_____	_____

Make lists of what's "likely" and "unlikely" for each fear you have. You'll be sure of some of your answers. With others, you might need expert advice on what is likely/unlikely. It might be a question of property or custody rights. Or about getting welfare assistance or job training.

Expert advice isn't always expensive. In some cities there are low-cost services. Call these places to ask about free or low-cost services:

- a shelter or women's center
- Legal Services
- County Bar Association (lawyers' group)
- a crisis hot line

Be sure to mention that you've been battered. There are sometimes special services for abused women.

Gather as much information as you can. Then return to

your "Worst Fears" lists. Make any changes your new information suggests.

WHAT'S THE WORST THAT CAN HAPPEN IF YOU STAY WITH THE MAN?

Think about the worst that might happen if you stay with your man. Think of what might happen short-term and long-term. If you have children, how will staying affect them? Consider emotional as well as physical harm.

After she left, Hope saw how much her children had suffered. It made her feel sad to remember.

"I'd say to my boy, 'Don't cry when Dad is home.' He was about five. I didn't know about being mentally battered. He mentally battered my boy."

Think back to the last time you were abused. *List* the things you were afraid of, starting with the worst. Were you afraid you might be killed? Crippled for life? What if you killed your man, as some abused women have? How would you feel later? If you have children, how would it affect them?

Try to imagine your future if any of these things happened. Do you get enough from the relationship to take such risks?

LOOKING AT BOTH SIDES

"Should I stay?" "Should I leave? " List the good things and the bad things about staying and about leaving.

*

Activity 4   *Leaving and Staying: The Good and the Bad of Each*

	Leaving		Staying	
	Good	*Bad*	*Good*	*Bad*
1.	————	————	————	————
2.	————	————	————	————
3.	————	————	————	————
4.	————	————	————	————
5.	————	————	————	————
6.	————	————	————	————
7.	————	————	————	————
8.	————	————	————	————
9.	————	————	————	————
10.	————	————	————	————

You may find that some items turn up on both lists. For instance, you might put "loneliness" on the "Bad" list under "Leaving." But you might know that you'll be lonely if you stay, too. But "seeing my friends" is unlikely to appear on both "Good" lists. And seeing your friends can do a lot to make you less lonely.

When you have finished the list, you may still be undecided. If so, score each *good* item you've written on a scale from 1 to 10. Number 10 will be the most important item. The least important item will be marked number 1. Do the same thing for the *bad* items. Then add the scores for the *good* items and the *bad* items. That should help you decide what you want to do.

The next step will be finding out *how* to do it.

WHAT CAN YOU DO IF YOU STAY?

Perhaps you've decided you can't leave just yet. You don't have skills for the job market. You have no supportive people in your life. Your children are not yet in school. You feel you have to take a chance on staying a while longer.

If you're serious about leaving later, you'll have to make some changes now. Make a friend. Join a support group. Get job skills through on-the-job training, classes, or volunteer work. Otherwise, you'll be in the same position later as you are now.

Some men bully only those who are afraid of them. You may be able to do some "forbidden" things by just *doing* them. However, it's a risk. Plan an emergency escape to a safe place before you take that risk. (See below.)

Many men are sorry right after they've battered. This is sometimes called "the honeymoon period." They're willing to give in to some things you want. This is a good time to get out of the house and meet people. It's a good time to start the changes you plan.

It may be hard to face new people with a black eye. Try to make yourself do it, anyway. Once your bruises fade, it's easy for your man to forget what he did. You won't be able to count on his being sorry. You'll be afraid of being hit again, if you try something new.

HOW TO PLAN FOR AN EMERGENCY ESCAPE

Whether you leave or stay, you'll be safer if you have an escape plan.

Learn to know the signs of coming violence, if you can. Do they begin weeks before the actual abuse, or only hours? Or minutes? *Write down the signs*. Write down changes in the way he acts, or in his tone of voice. This will help to get you into action before the violence starts. You won't be so likely to tell yourself: "Oh, I'm just imagining things."

Where can you go for safety? The best choice is to the home of someone who cares for you. Someone who will support you, no matter what you do. This might be a good friend or a relative. Otherwise, choose a hotel/motel *ahead of time*. Practice getting there from your house when you're not under stress. You should also be prepared with these things:

- money for cab fare
- change of clothes for yourself and/or children (hide clothes away from home, at a neighbor's house, or at your job)
- money for one or more nights at a motel
- extra house key and car key
- list of emergency phone numbers

Plan for a quick getaway, day or night. Find excuses to go outdoors that won't make him suspicious. Make a habit of taking out the garbage at midnight. Or walking the dog twice a day.

When you need to escape, pretend you're going to do one of those tasks. Once outside, just keep going. Get into the car and drive off quickly. Or keep walking until you get to a phone.

If you have children, make plans for taking them. Plan to tell the man you hear the baby crying. If you can, pick her/him up and exit from a back door or window. Prepare older children to go to a neighbor's house if you can't get away. They can call the police. Officers may help you leave with younger children.

If you must leave without the children, go back for them. Return to the house with a police officer as soon as you can. Or pick them up at school. Your right to custody can be endangered if they are not with you.

PREPARING TO LEAVE PERMANENTLY

After you have an emergency plan, you can think about leaving for good. If you plan to *stay away*, here are some practical things to think about.

Protect Your Money and Property

Laws about property rights for married people are different from state to state. They are also different for people who just live together. You'll need a lawyer's advice on what a court might award you. Also, on what things you can legally take with you. You then need to plan how to get the things out.

Remove as many personal belongings as you can several weeks before you leave. Include family photographs and sentimental objects, if you want them. Those are the things he might destroy.

Try to take important items to a friend for safe-keeping. This may be too risky if the man notices everything you do. If he does, make a list of important things you want to take. (Don't forget items important to your children.) Move them little by little to two or three places in the house. Then you'll be able to pack them more quickly when you do leave.

Remove your things when your partner isn't at home. Try to have a friend with you, in case he returns. Find out whether the police can be there. There may also be other community agencies that can help you.

Unless a lawyer says you can't, take half the money in checking accounts. Do the same with savings accounts. Don't leave your share of money in joint accounts to take out later. Once you've left, your partner may withdraw all money from the accounts. He may take your name off credit cards. He may change all the locks on the doors. You could find yourself with no money or property twenty-four hours after you leave.

It's possible you don't know exactly what you and he jointly own. Look for papers that show stocks, property, loans, insurance policies you both own. Write down all the information. If you can do it safely, xerox the papers. If necessary, give all papers and lists to a friend you trust.

It isn't mean or unfair to take what is yours. Don't deprive yourself or your children of what you need because of guilt feelings.

Plan Where To Go

Try to find a place to live before you leave. It might be one of these places:

- a battered women's shelter
- a friend or relative's home
- a Safe Home for abused women
- an apartment of your own

There are now battered women's shelters and Safe Homes in many communities. Chapter 15 tells how to find out about them.

Try to decide where you want to live permanently. You might want to move to a different city. Sometimes a local shelter can help you find temporary shelter in a new city. Check housing ads so you'll know what to expect in your price range. You may need public housing or welfare assistance. Find out what papers you'll need to show you qualify. Get them together to take with you.

The better you prepare now, the easier it will be for you later.

Chapter 8

Getting Professional Help: The Problem of Sexism

"Professionals" are people who have been trained in a special field. They might be lawyers, police, or prosecutors. They might be counselors or doctors.

Professionals can be very helpful to you. They can increase your safety. They can guide you through the legal system. They can help you get your rights. They can help you face problems and make changes in your life.

Professionals can also make things worse for you. Not all of them are good at their work. Some are good, but may not give you the kind of help you need. Their ideas about women might even be harmful to you.

In Chapter 1, you read about the "male image" and the "female image." These images teach us to expect different things of males and females. Those differing expectations are called *sexism*.

Sexism is the belief that:

- males and females are born with completely different traits
- males are superior to females
- men have the right to make decisions and laws that rule women's lives

All of us have sexist ideas, to some degree. Women can be just as sexist as men. However, a male professional who is sexist may be a special problem for a woman. Because he's a male, he may think he's more capable than you. He may think that even about things that have nothing to do with his work. He'll want to make decisions that should be yours. He'll want to take over more than you need him to.

You may agree with him that women don't know how to do things well. If you think that, you might feel helpless. But it isn't good for you to feel helpless, and you don't need to. Maybe it's true that you don't know much about law, or counseling. But you are beginning to know what you want. You have a right to make your own decisions—and your own mistakes. That's how you learn what you want and what you can do.

Some professionals take advantage of their clients. For example, a male therapist (counselor) may try to have sex with a woman client. He may tell her that sex with him will be good for her. Having sex with a client is unethical and sometimes illegal. Woman clients are nearly always hurt by these relationships.

For all these reasons, it's usually best for you to hire a female professional. Try to find one who knows about battering. Try finding one who is as nonsexist as possible. She should, of course, be good at her work. She also needs to be someone you can afford.

Sometimes it won't be you who is paying the professional. You may be using a professional who is paid by the government. It might be a prosecutor, a police officer, or a welfare worker. But you're entitled to good services, whether you're paying or not. You are also entitled to respect. You'll need to make it clear that you expect both.

The next two chapters will help you get what you need from professionals.

Chapter 9

Getting Help From Police and Prosecutors

This chapter will help you decide what you want from police and prosecutors. Suppose you don't get what you want? You'll also find some ideas on what to do about that.

POLICE ASSISTANCE
Should You Call the Police?

Lynn remembers the thoughts she had about calling the police:

"The police? In the black community? My God, that's the ultimate enemy! Don't call the police over here, they'll probably beat you up, drag your man off and throw him in jail for three hundred years!

"But Ann, who worked at the legal service agency, thought it was important to call them and follow through—for myself, and because it's going to help other women in the long run. And I knew he wasn't going to jail. He was just going to have to go to counseling."

Try to decide beforehand whether you'll call the police next time you're attacked. If you do call them, what will you want them to do? Will you want them to stop the attack and calm the man down? Arrest him? Take him away? Take you to a safe place?

Try to find out how likely you are to get what you want.

Police practices vary from one place to another. In some places, police won't give much help in a battering case. In others, they're very helpful. They will take victims to a shelter or a hospital. They will give careful advice on how to follow through with a case.

Find out what to expect from your local police. Call one of these agencies:

- a shelter for battered women
- a women's rights group
- the County Bar Association

If you do decide you'll call the police, practice now what to say. Make it clear that it's an emergency, and give your address. "I'm being beaten up. I'm at 628 Borden Street." Don't say it's your husband or boyfriend who's attacking you.

HOW TO GET THE BEST RESPONSE FROM POLICE

1. Be as calm as possible.
2. Don't be afraid to ask the police to make a report.
3. Tell them about the assault in detail.
4. Show them any injuries, bruises, or damaged property.
5. Let them know if anyone saw the attack.
6. Let them know if the man has hit you before this.
7. Show them "no contact" or "restraining" orders, if you have them.
8. Ask them for phone numbers of shelters, hot lines, prosecutors, and counselors.
9. You may want to follow up on the case. Ask for the case number of the report and a phone number. If you don't hear from them, the case number will be important when you call.

WHEN WILL POLICE MAKE AN ARREST?

Police must have good reason to believe a crime has been committed. Then they can make a legal arrest. There must be some evidence of the crime. The evidence could be a bloody nose or other injury. They will probably make an arrest if one of these things is true:

1. Your state has a law that says police have to arrest when there is an assault. (This is called "mandatory arrest.")
2. He can be arrested for something else he may have done. This means there is a "warrant" for his arrest. If you know there is a warrant, tell the police.
3. The assault was very serious, involving a weapon or a major injury.
4. The abuser attacks the police or attacks you while police are present.

FOLLOWING THROUGH ON THE CASE

You may or may not want the case to go to court. Once you call police, the case might go to court. But it might not. The prosecutor decides whether or not it will. Prosecutors sometimes ask you what you want. But sometimes they just do whatever they think is best.

If the man is convicted of the charges, it can help you. The court can order him not to contact you for a certain period. The court could also order him to do any of these things:

- go to batterers' counseling
- get treatment for alcoholism
- pay for your medical treatment
- replace damaged or stolen property

Suppose you get back together with the man before he goes to court. He might try to get you to stop the prosecution. But you can't do that. Only the prosecutor or the judge can stop it. You can honestly tell the man it's out of your hands.

Thinking It Through

If *you* want the charges dropped, you can tell the prosecutor. He or she may be willing to drop the case. But it's important to think through your reasons for doing this.

Have you cooperated in pressing charges before, and did you follow through? Did you get the results you wanted? Or did you feel let down or betrayed by the system? Perhaps the courts were less responsive to abused women than they've become now. Or the state laws may have changed. Find out whether there have been important changes in your area. Call women's groups or Legal Services for information.

Perhaps you wanted to get him into court the first time you called the police. You were angry. Then your feelings changed. You decided you still loved the man. The idea of "putting him in jail" made you feel guilty. Or maybe you were afraid a jail term would make him furious with you. That could mean worse violence once he was out. And you didn't know of a safe place to go.

What if you again decide, "I still love him"? Will you go through with it anyway, this time? Can you hold out if your man sweet-talks or threatens you? What about guilt; what about fears of worse violence? Can you handle all that better now? Maybe not. But if you prepare for it, you might be able to.

Find out where you can get help. The prosecutor's office may have a special program to help you. Or a shelter may have one. Many shelters now have "legal advocates." They are people who will advise you about ways the law can help you. They will go to court with you.

You can also ask for a friend's help. Your friend can go with you every time you go to court. Your friend can also go with you each time the prosecutor interviews you.

Find out about these things in advance. Also find out about safe places to stay, in case the man becomes violent. Call shelters and women's groups.

There are other ways you can prepare, too. Ask a friend to "role-play" possible situations with you. Have her pretend that she is your man or the prosecutor. Ask her to try to make you feel guilty or unsure. Try to answer her as you really would answer the prosecutor. Keep doing it until you're not afraid. Then decide whether you still want to ask the prosecutor to drop charges.

PROSECUTION

Suppose you don't ask the prosecutor to drop charges. That doesn't mean the case will go to court. Or that if it does, the man will be convicted or punished. The prosecutor may decide not to take the case to court for one of these reasons:

- your injuries are not serious
- the man says he didn't intend to hurt you
- there is little evidence
- there is no record of other assaults or other crimes
- the prosecutor is afraid of losing the case

Success at trial also depends on a number of factors. Here are some of them:

- how convincing the evidence is (including the witnesses)

- whether the judge really believes battering is a crime
- how hard the prosecutor was willing and able to work on the case
- whether there are programs for men who batter
- whether the man seems to be sorry
- whether the man seems to be a "solid citizen"

Like other people, prosecutors have their own values. These values—including sexist attitudes—often affect what they do. This may be the case even when they believe they are being fair.

All of these things will affect what happens in your case. Some of them are beyond your control. But that doesn't mean you shouldn't try to influence what happens.

Dealing with the Prosecutor

You may think that the prosecutor isn't taking your case seriously. Nothing is ever explained to you. Your phone calls aren't returned. You can't tell what—if anything—is happening.

Let the prosecutor know that you're not satisfied. You may be told that it can't be helped, that the office is understaffed. This is often true. The prosecutor has many cases besides yours.

You might get support and information on the court process somewhere else. Contact women's organizations. (For example: YWCA's, the local chapter of the National Organization for Women, a shelter.) One of them might even pressure the prosecutor to keep you better informed.

If you still think you're getting the runaround, ask for a different prosecutor. Or ask to speak to his or her supervisor. If you complain, you might get a better prosecutor. Or you might get nowhere. It depends on how your particular prosecutor's office is run. Find out all you can about your prosecutor's office from women's groups. It may help you decide how far you'll go in fighting your case.

HOW CAN YOU KEEP THE ABUSER AWAY?

Is the man your boyfriend, former lover, or divorced husband? If so, you don't need a legal order to keep him away. You have all the rights you'd have if he were a stranger. You can charge him with a crime if he does any of these things:

- enters your house without permission
- forces you to have sex with him
- assaults or threatens you

The charge might be trespassing, rape, or assault. Call the district court to find out what charge you can legally make.

Are you married to the man, or do you have a child by him? If so, you may need a legal order to keep him away. Terms for such orders differ from place to place. The terms include: *no contact order; temporary restraining order; order of protection.*

For some orders, you don't need to consult a lawyer or a prosecutor. Call your County Bar Association, district court, or a shelter. Ask what the proper order is called. Ask how you go about getting it.

By itself, the order probably won't keep the man away. You'll need to call the police every time he violates it. You'll need to follow through each time with calls to the prosecutor. If he's sure he's going to be punished, he might stay away.

Chapter 10

Getting Help From Lawyers and Counselors

DO YOU NEED TO HIRE A LAWYER?

You may need a lawyer if you are:

• ending a marriage
• separating from the father of your child/children

A lawyer will probably cost you money. There are some free legal services for abused women. But they are rare. To find out what your community offers, call:

• Legal Services
• County Bar Association
• City or County Prosecutor's office
• women's organizations

BEFORE YOU SEE A LAWYER

Try to find a lawyer with experience in wife-abuse cases. The organizations listed above may suggest names, if you ask. Ask friends, too.

Before you see a lawyer, try to decide what you want. You may both love and hate your husband. That might make you feel mixed up. It's not a lawyer's business to help you sort out your feelings. And you'll be charged for the time you spend talking about them.

If you can't sort out your feelings by yourself, a counselor might help. But first, try to answer these questions:

1. Do you want a divorce? This question might be very hard for you to face. To help think it through, read Chapters 1–7 again. Look again at your fears. How do you feel about loneliness? What about needing love? What about money and support of children?

2. If you want a divorce, is this the right time? Will your anger enable you to go through with it? If it fades, will you back out? If so, you'll be at square one. And you'll also have a lawyer's bill.

CHILD CUSTODY

One of the most difficult legal problems is child custody. When the father is violent, it's even harder. So, it may be helpful to ask yourself more questions.

1. Do you want custody of the children? Are you afraid your husband might keep you from getting it? Has he threatened to keep you from getting it?

There may be reasons for your fears. Is your husband an important person in a small community? Do you have a history of mental illness? Emotional problems? Drug, alcohol, or child abuse? A criminal record?

Don't assume it's hopeless, even if some of your answers are yes. Those things might make it hard for you to get custody. But you won't know until you talk to a lawyer. Meanwhile, try not to let your husband know you're afraid. He might just be bluffing.

Consult with a lawyer who knows the community and its judges. There are things you can do to make a good case for yourself. A good lawyer can advise you about that. He or she can also advise you about your chances of winning custody. However,until the case has gone to court, no one can be sure.

Perhaps you have reason to believe you haven't been a

responsible parent. Now is a good time to begin changes. Enroll in parenting classes. Join AA. Do community volunteer work. You can establish yourself as a good parent and citizen. It may be much easier when you're not afraid of being battered.

2. What might happen if you give up custody?

Maybe you don't want custody. But you're afraid of what might happen if you give it up. How will your child react? How will that affect you? Will the child be safe? How often will you be able to see the child?

A shelter or hot line worker can help you with some of these questions. She may be able to help you reduce the risks to your child and you.

You might change your mind about custody later. Right now, you may feel that you can barely take care of yourself. In a few months, you may feel much better. You may want the children with you then. But you may not be able to get them from their father. If you're not sure what to do, wait. Don't give up custody now.

Think about help you might get if you kept the children. You don't have to do everything all by yourself. Help may be available from nursery schools or day care centers. Friends and family may help. Agencies such as child protective services may help. Counselors may give you support you need.

Think calmly about your options before you decide about custody. Give yourself a chance to weather the crisis. Whatever decision you make then, it will be a better one.

SHOULD YOU SEE A COUNSELOR?

Women who have been abused face many problems. Some of these are emotional. Chapter 11 discusses ways you can deal with these problems yourself. Friends and family can help, too. Even so, you may want to talk to a professional counselor or therapist.

Your counselor must be someone who understands battering. She must know how much danger you are in. Then she can help you decide whether or not to leave your partner. And she can help you stick to whatever decision you make.

Lou's husband beat her because she had so many faults. At least, that's what Lou thought until she saw a therapist. She says:

"In the first part of our marriage, he beat me because he was ashamed of me. In the last part, it was because I was controlling his mind. I went to see a psychiatrist. He said, 'Lady, your problem is that you think you have a problem. Your *husband* needs to see me.'

"That was the first time I thought it was something he was doing rather than what I was doing. After I saw the therapist I started to think, 'Maybe it's not all me.'"

FINDING A COUNSELOR

Ask friends and co-workers if they know of good counselors. Ask what they liked about them and what problems they were helpful with.

In a big city, you may find special counseling services for women. There may be special services for abused women. Also, there may be agencies that don't charge much if people have little money.

Look in the telephone book yellow pages under:

- Social Services
- Social Work
- Psychology
- Therapy

Look in the white pages under:

- Abuse
- Battering
- Women

- Feminist
- Rape Counseling
- Child Abuse

Settle down for an hour or two of phone calls. You'll be referred to other telephone numbers. You'll get taped messages. You'll be told that so-and-so will return your call. You won't be able to get an appointment with one quick call.

You may find yourself putting off making these calls. That's not unusual. Most people are nervous about calling a counselor.

When you do call, have pencil and paper ready. Write down the counselor's name and the fee. Add other notes, including how you feel about the counselor.

CHOOSING A COUNSELOR

It's important to choose a counselor who is not sexist. (See Chapter 8.) A sexist counselor won't help you build the self-confidence you need. A sexist counselor may also convince you that being abused is your fault. She or he could lead you right back to the man.

How can you know if a counselor has sexist attitudes? To find out, you will have to ask questions. Ask them at your first meeting, or even before, on the telephone. Try these:

- How do you feel about how women's and men's roles have been changing?
- Do you think mothers of small children should work outside the home?
- Should the one who earns the money make most of the household decisions?

The answers won't tell you everything. But you'll be

able to tell which way the counselor leans. You'll be able to avoid a counselor who thinks women have few rights. Or that men have the right to "discipline" their wives.

Advantages of a Woman Counselor

A woman is more likely to understand your feelings about the violent man. She may get you in touch with supportive women's groups. A male counselor is less likely to know about such groups. In addition, a female counselor can be a good role model for you.

Some counselors focus on saving a relationship—even an abusive one. They don't see how dangerous abusers are. They don't realize that the abuser is the one who must change. They may blame the victim as much as her abuser. A woman counselor is less likely to see things that way. But don't take it for granted. Ask her: "Do you think that only one partner can be at fault for battering? Or is it always both partners?"

Your counselor may think the problem is the way the two partners interact. She may think that they have equal responsibility for the abuse. If so, you'll be safer looking for a different counselor. Find someone who understands that *only* the person who batters can stop it.

HOW HELPFUL IS YOUR COUNSELOR?

At the beginning, you and the counselor should agree on goals. Use these goals to measure how much progress the counselor has helped you make.

For instance, you may still feel unhappy after two months of counseling. But your original goal was to learn more about what makes you tick. Or it was to learn to express your emotions. If any of that has happened, you've made progress.

But maybe your goal was to increase your self-respect.

Yet whenever you see the counselor, you feel worse about yourself. If so, something is definitely wrong.

Tell the counselor you're not satisfied. An ethical counselor will try to find out what's wrong. She'll try to strike a balance of responsibility between the two of you. She'll try to find better ways you can work together.

But what if the counselor doesn't agree that you're not working well together? Ask her to tell you what signs of progress she sees. Her answers may be clear. They may make you see how she's helped you. If they don't, it may be time to stop seeing her.

It's hard to tell a counselor you want to stop seeing her. But remember, you're buying services. If you don't get what you want, you have a right to leave. Be honest with the counselor about your reasons. She may suggest other counselors who would be better for you.

At this point, don't tell yourself: "I tried counseling, and it didn't work." Keep "shopping" until you find a counselor you can work with. With luck, you'll find one who will help you to help yourself.

Chapter 11

You Can Be Your Own Counselor

Professionals can be lifesavers at times. But sooner or later, it's up to you to help yourself.

Right now, you may feel that you are the last person you can count on. You feel confused. Depressed. Uncertain of what you want to do. Your will to act seems paralyzed. Sometimes you think you're going crazy.

None of that needs to last forever. You *can* help yourself, even while you're still confused. You've already begun—by reading this book.

You can begin to make changes in the way you think and feel about yourself. Through these changes, you can find the strength to act.

CHANGING THE WAY YOU TALK TO YOURSELF

An abused woman gets a lot of verbal abuse. Usually a woman can't take this for long without being affected. She begins to agree with what's being said about her. She starts saying the same things to herself.

All of us give ourselves messages. We can give ourselves messages that help us. But we can also say things to ourselves that lead to failure:

"You don't deserve nice clothes. You're too fat and ugly."

"You're helpless and stupid and can't take care of yourself."

"Nothing is ever going to turn out right for you."

If you give yourself messages like these, your life probably won't get better. You may promise yourself that you'll make it better. But you also go on telling yourself that you're a hopeless mess. So if you're hopeless, how can you make your life better?

You can begin by changing the messages you give yourself. Maybe you can't change the abuser. But at least you can stop abusing *yourself!* The exercises below will help you treat yourself better.

WHAT ARE YOU TELLING YOURSELF?

It's important that you put your thoughts on paper. That way, you can *see* your thoughts. Seeing them will help you face them and do something about them. If they remain silent, you might pretend they aren't there, or don't matter.

List your self-criticisms exactly as you think them: "Dummy!" "Oh, my god, you screwed up again." Some may be single words: "fat," "ugly," "stupid," "hopeless." Others may be whole sentences or paragraphs:

"You dimwit! You really are a hopeless fool. You ruin everything you touch. You never learn. You keep saying you'll reform, but you won't. You're ugly. You're fat, too, because you don't have any willpower."

Activity 5   Self-criticism List

1. _____

2. _____

3. _____

4. _____

5. _____

6. _____

7. _____

8. _____

9. _____

10. _____

You may talk to yourself this way, silently, often. And it's even worse than if another person were doing it. Other people speak to you out loud. You know what they say. You can talk back. But if the criticisms are silent, you may never answer them. They go on tearing you down.

Once you know what you're saying to yourself, you can change it. The next section deals with that.

GENERAL STATEMENTS AND FACTUAL STATEMENTS

Many of your self-criticisms are general statements. A general statement is about the kind of person you think you are. An example would be: "You're stupid."

A factual statement is about a particular fact. It may be something you did. Examples would be: "You made a mistake," or "You overslept." It may be about something that happened. For example: "Your car broke down."

The two kinds of statements have very different effects. "You're stupid" leaves no room for change. Compare that with the statement: "You made a mistake." This statement allows for the possibility that you are not stupid. You can change the way you act and what you do. Even smart people do stupid things from time to time. Everybody makes mistakes.

The following exercise will help you replace general statements with factual ones. It first gives an example in which a woman does these things:

1. Accuses herself of being stupid.
2. Writes it down.
3. Analyzes the self-criticism and sees that it refers to one fact.
4. States what happened: she burned the toast.

Write down your own statements. Then replace them with what actually happened.

Activity 6   *Replacement List*

Self-critical statement	**What happened**
1. You're sure stupid!	*burned the toast*
2. Oh, my god, you're never going to change. You'll always be a fat, useless slob.	*ate double ice cream cone*
3. _____	_____
_____	
_____	
4. _____	_____
_____	
_____	
5. _____	_____
_____	
_____	

A simple statement of "what happened" isn't a statement of blame. It reduces the guilt, anxiety, and depression that go with self-blame.

Doing the exercise can help free you from self-blame. Then you can think clearly about the behavior you don't like. You can think of ways to change the things you do.

Do the exercise every day. Replace every general statement with a fact. Keep doing it until you can do it without
even trying. This may take several weeks. But after a while,
your inner talk will change. It may go something like this:

"Well, fatty, you did it again!... Whoops! I mean...
let's see, what did I do? Correction: I had potatoes and
gravy."

Before long, you'll be skipping right over the "Well,
fatty" remarks. You'll replace them with a simple statement
of what you ate.

WHAT DID YOU DO RIGHT TODAY?

Abused women often find it hard to think of anything
they've done right. How can you get control over your life,
if you do nothing right? You need to start noticing the
things you do that deserve credit.

Here are some ideas about what you can take credit for:

Making things better for someone else. Did you listen
to someone's troubles? Control your temper with your
child? Shop for a sick friend? Prepare a meal? Smile at
someone who looked lonely?

Starting to get more control over your life. Did you
make a decision? Make a phone call to get information?
Begin learning to drive? Stay away from a destructive person?

Making yourself feel better. Did you take time to look at
the sunset? Take a long bubble bath? Walk for the fun of it?
Play cards with a good friend? Go out to listen to music?

Make a list of all the things you did right today. They
don't have to be a big deal. When you're feeling low, a
small effort is worth a lot.

Suppose today you decided to take up jogging. Maybe
you didn't get any farther than one block. But you got up off
your chair. You got some exercise. You made a step in the

direction of change. You deserve to give yourself credit for that.

Each item you add to your list will strengthen you. The list shows that you've already done some worthwhile things. You'll gain courage to try more of them. You'll begin to get a sense of what is possible.

Chris discovered she was accomplishing a great deal. A kick in the head by her husband had given her epilepsy. But she went to school, and took care of her two preschool children.

"One day I was thinking, I'm not good for nothing, and then I thought, well, just what have I done today? I started writing it down, and I had half a page of stuff... I did the laundry and the dishes, went to school all day.... You add it all up and, 'Oh, gosh, you're doing it, you're making it.'"

Chapter 12

A Courageous Act A Day

A courageous act is any worthwhile thing you do in spite of being afraid. Worthwhile simply means an activity worth doing. It might be asking a friend to come to dinner. It might be looking for a job or an apartment.

You may think that "little" things like these aren't courageous acts. You think courage means "big" things, like saving a drowning person. Yet you may be afraid to do those "little" things yourself. But you don't like to admit it.

DENYING YOUR FEARS

It's not strange that you don't like to admit feeling scared. Such feelings are painful. You hope that if you deny having them, they'll go away.

But most of the time, they won't go away. You don't become less anxious by denying the way you feel. You just put off doing whatever it is that makes you feel anxious. It goes like this:

"I shouldn't be nervous about a little thing like apartment hunting. So I'm *not* nervous. I'm just not doing it today because I think I'm getting a cold. I'll do it tomorrow." And when tomorrow comes, you say, "I couldn't look for an apartment because I missed the bus. I'll go tomorrow."

Those are not reasons. They're excuses. Excuses explain why it's *hard* to do something. They don't explain why you didn't *do* it.

When you keep putting off doing something, listen carefully to your explanations. Are they good reasons for putting it off? Or are they really excuses? Okay, you missed the bus. Why didn't you take the next bus? Don't use this question to blame yourself. Use it to understand what's really going on.

If you're making excuses, you're probably trying to hide your fears from yourself. To find out if that's what you're doing, try this. Ask yourself if you really mean "couldn't." "Couldn't" often means "didn't want to." That often means "I was too scared, but didn't want to admit it."

If you continue to deny your fears, you can go on putting things off. But when you admit your fears, you can make yourself rise above them. That takes courage. In the following pages, you'll learn ways you can increase your courage.

TAKING THE FIRST STEPS

Suppose you've been telling yourself you'll go out and get a job. Or you've told yourself you'll rent an apartment, or make a new friend. But then you think how you'll feel if you don't get what you want. You're afraid you will feel like a failure. Then you get depressed. So you keep putting it off. You don't do it.

You have put yourself through "failure." And yet you haven't tried!

You need to think about your plans differently. Think only in terms of what you know you can do. "I'm going to *look* for a job or an apartment." "I'm going to *invite* someone in for coffee."

This may seem like a small difference. But it is important. You can't control what other people do. But you can control *your* part of the action. If you don't get the job, you don't have to blame yourself. You tried hard. You can give yourself credit for that.

Choose your task with care. Make it one you're willing and able to carry out. Be clear about exactly what you want to do. Afterward, be clear about whether or not you did it. If you didn't do it all, did you do some of it? If not, figure out why. Once you know that, you can work on changes. And give yourself credit for the part you *did* do.

Maybe you decided to go to a community college. But you kept putting off applying. Day after day you put off filling out the forms. You ask yourself why. And you answer that you're afraid you'll flunk out. You haven't been in school for fifteen years.

It will help if you stop thinking about taking hard courses. There may be easy ones to take first. Sometimes there are even courses for people who have been out of school for years.

Think about the *first* thing you have to do. Maybe you need to talk to a college counselor. If that seems too hard, choose something easier. It might be talking to a friend who's a student. Maybe it's walking through the campus, noticing how many older students there are.

Break the task down into small steps. Choose a first step you *know* you can take. Then be sure you take it.

TAKE CREDIT FOR EACH COURAGEOUS ACT

Give yourself credit for the hard things you do. You probably find it easy to tell others they're doing well. You give credit to those around you—husband, lover, children, friends. But you find it hard to take credit for yourself. Many women are like that. But you don't need to be.

Make up your mind to treat yourself well. Don't say, "I

don't deserve it." You deserve good treatment, just like anyone else.

Review "What Did You Do Right Today?" in Chapter 11. When you value yourself, others will value you. Start taking credit now and start giving yourself rewards.

BE GOOD TO YOURSELF

Being good to yourself means giving yourself rewards for courageous acts. It also means allowing yourself pleasures for no special reason. Either way, you have to know what things make you feel good.

See how many pleasures you can think of. Some should be pleasures that are easily available. Maybe you love to listen to music, but you seldom let yourself. Start being good to yourself right now, and play your favorite record.

Don't be afraid to plan ahead for bigger pleasures, too. Suppose you want a long vacation by yourself or with another adult. If you have children, that may be an impossible dream for now. But with careful planning, you may be able to go away for a weekend. That would be a start toward your big dream.

It's sometimes painful to be aware of all the things you want. It's hard when you don't have the time or money for them. Yet it's important not to lose sight of what you want. Because unless you know what you want, you can't begin to get it.

Find Out What Would Give You Pleasure

Make three lists: 1) pleasures you enjoy and want more of; 2) pleasures you used to have (at any time in your life); and 3) things you might like but have never tried (herbal tea, gardening, mystery novels, bowling). Don't forget small pleasures. Do you like reading in bed? Watching a plant grow? Putting up a shelf? Be sure to include those.

Activity 7 A   Pleasures List

Pleasures I Enjoy	Pleasures I Used to Have	Pleasures I Might Like to Have
Watering Plants	*Roller Skating*	*Writing poetry*
Talking to friends	*Sewing*	*Camping*

_____

_____

_____

_____

_____

_____

Put a check next to pleasures you might have in the next week. Include those that need planning ahead or getting information. Be sure there are some you can get right away. And that don't cost anything. Do you have at least ten? If not, go back and see what you can add.

Make a list of pleasant events you can look forward to. Include a pleasant event for each part of the day.

Activity 7 B: Daily Pleasures

Morning	Afternoon	Evening
Watch sunrise	*Lunch with co-worker (Ann)*	*Telephone (Sue)*
Water plants	*Sew*	*Write poetry*

_____

_____

_____

_____

_____

_____

_____

_____

Your list shows that you can have some pleasures in life. You can wake up each morning with things to look forward to.

Diane was surprised to learn how many things she enjoyed doing alone.

"I guess I thought I would die from loneliness, but I really don't need somebody to keep me entertained. I've got my books, I've got my stereo...."

TAKE CARE OF YOUR PHYSICAL SELF

It's important to take good care of your body. If you don't feel well, it can make you feel depressed. It can also make it hard for you to think clearly. Everything you do is affected by your body.

Eat well. Stay away from junk food. If you must have something sweet, buy or fix something really special. Let yourself plan it and enjoy it without feeling guilty. Otherwise, eat what's good for you and take the time to enjoy it. Don't eat on the run and don't skip meals.

Sleep well. Try to get about eight hours of sleep each night. If you have trouble sleeping, try to start relaxing an hour before bedtime. If it doesn't work, don't toss and turn. Pass the time enjoyably. Listen to soothing music. Read something light. Stretch and rest without trying to sleep.

Don't panic if you're not getting a regular good night's sleep. You won't fall apart. Don't tell yourself, "I've got to sleep tonight or I'll fall apart." That will make it even harder to relax and sleep.

If you feel tired most of the time, see a doctor. If you get sleeping pills, don't use them more than a month. A doctor might not tell you whether or not the pills are addictive. They can also have dangerous side effects. Drinking alcohol to fall asleep can be a dangerous habit, too.

Exercise. Exercise will make you feel and look better. Concentrate on the pleasure of moving your body. If you're out of shape, start slowly. Stay with it only as long as it feels good. If you stop while you're enjoying it, you'll probably do it again. Follow this principle whether you run, swim, do sit-ups, or join a team. It will help you to make exercise a regular part of your life.

Look well. The way you look affects the way you feel. Don't give yourself a chance to feel sloppy. Fix your hair. Put on whatever make-up you usually wear. Do these things even if you're not leaving the house or seeing anyone. It's a way of reminding yourself that *you* care about you.

Chapter 13

Steps to Finding Friends

Abusive men often demand that their partners give up other relationships. So, by now, you may have few or no friends.

You may think that friends can't give you much, compared with a lover. It's true that there are differences between what each can give. But some of the differences exist only in our minds. We *think* that only sexual relationships can be intimate and caring. So we place limits on what to expect of friends. We can change that attitude, if we want to.

Lynn has advice for women who have been isolated by abusive men:

"When you feel lonely, instead of looking for a man, you can go with some women to hear music. . . . If I hadn't left, I wouldn't have known all these great women."

WHY AREN'T ACQUAINTANCES FRIENDS?

Often, women don't see the flaws in people they hope will become lovers. Yet they find many things "wrong" with people who might become friends. If that's what you do, you can begin to change now. You can change the way you look at people who might become friends.

A lonely person may find fault with everyone. She may

feel that nobody would want her for a friend. So she rejects people before they have a chance to reject her.

Is this something you do? To find out, list ten people you see from time to time. Include people you work with or see in the neighbohood. Include those you see at church, school, and where you do your shopping. Include relatives and former friends. Then complete the exercise below.

Activity 8　*Why Aren't Acquaintances Friends?*

1. *Mary*　　*sister-in-law; lives in another city*
2. *Betty*　　*neighbor; gossips too much*
3. _____
4. _____
5. _____
6. _____
7. _____
8. _____
9. _____
10. _____

Do you think some of these people might become a friend? If so, you have a good pool to draw from. If not, you have a problem to solve.

Did you mostly write down things you don't like about the ten people? If so, notice whether you wrote general statements, like "stupid," "nosey," "a fool."

If you did that, you might want to change the pattern. Turn back to Activity 6 in Chapter 11. Now follow the same method to replace the statements above. Change general statements to facts. "She's a fool" will become "She giggles when she's nervous." Practice this method. After a while, the put-downs will be replaced by simple descriptions. Then you can decide whether the person's flaws are really important.

Don't pass up a chance at a friendship by being too critical. Take a chance with a few people. If you spend a little time with them, you might be less lonely. Pay attention to how you feel about yourself when you're with them. If they make you feel bad, try someone else.

Find people you can enjoy talking with over a cup of coffee. Or someone you'll spend half an hour with, after a movie or bowling. She needn't be someone you think will become your best friend. But you need to start someplace. It takes time to make friends. And you can't always tell at first who you will like.

After a while, some acquaintances will become good friends. Then, if you meet a new man, you can take it slow. You won't feel you *have* to have a man. You'll have friends to be with—friends who care about you. Romance can then be something you *want*. It won't be something you'll die without. Your judgements about the men you become involved with can then become clearer.

After Nicole had a circle of friends, she said:

"I think a lot of black women [like me] want so much to feel good and to feel special by their man, that if he batters them, they say, 'Well, at least he loves me.' But now I know I don't need to have a man in my life to make me happy."

MEETING NEW PEOPLE

Start looking at everyone you meet as a possible friend. Even if you don't go many places, you meet a lot of people. You meet them at the grocery store or at the laundromat. You see them in the waiting room of your doctor's or dentist's office. Have you ever heard of anyone meeting an interesting man in such situations? Why not an interesting woman? You can use these situations for making friends, if you want to.

There are even easier places to find friends. Two of the best are classes and volunteer groups. At your job is another.

CLASSES, JOBS, VOLUNTEER GROUPS

Perhaps you need to learn some skills for a job. Or you need to pass a course to get into college. Taking a class may be important to your long-range plans. But classes also give you a chance to meet new people. Think about taking classes where you might find friends.

Look into all-women's classes. At least some of the women will also be there to find friends. And none of you will be trying to impress male classmates. You might want to start with a support group. The YWCA, the National Organization for Women, and some churches offer these.

At most colleges you will find a Women's Center. This is a good place to meet people and to get useful information. Find out about classes that are small and informal. They're better places for meeting people than big lecture courses.

If you're job hunting, pay attention to the people you'd be working with. Try to choose a workplace where you think you can find friends. If you're forty, you may feel isolated among workers in their twenties. The same goes for a five-person office where you're the only non-professional. Even so, you might meet people who could become friends. It depends on how open you are to different kinds of people.

If you have any extra time, do volunteer work. You will find interesting things to do. You'll meet people who care about the same things you do. Watch the newspaper for notices of where volunteers are needed. Or call United Way for the names of groups that want volunteers.

Look at every part of your life in terms of finding friends. You can end your isolation. If you're willing to use some thought and energy, you'll find the way.

Chapter 14

Reaching Out

So there you are. You're at the laundromat, on the job, or in a class. How do you make a new friend?

RISKING THE FIRST STEPS

To make friends, you must be willing to make the first move. That may be very hard. Why? Because you fear your friendly move may be rejected. But stop and think a minute. Will the sky really fall down if that happens?

Suppose you say something friendly, and the other person turns away. You might feel bad for a while. But that feeling doesn't have to last. You can put it out of your mind. And if the other person *is* friendly, you might make a friend. Isn't it worth the risk?

GETTING TO KNOW PEOPLE ON THE JOB

Let's suppose you're new on your job. Hardly anybody has spoken to you. You might think that's because nobody's interested in you. But have you done anything to let people know you're interested in *them*? You know you're shy, but they may think you're just unfriendly. You may need to start smiling, to start saying "Hello."

If you haven't been friendly so far, they may not smile back at first. It may take several tries before they'll risk being friendly to you.

Don't give up if your friendly action is rejected by one

person. Don't say to yourself: "They're all that way." "They're a bunch of snobs." "They all have lots of friends already."

If you hear yourself saying that, ask yourself what proof you have. How do you know they're *all* "that way"? Is it *all* of them—or just one? *List* the proofs you have that *all* of them are unfriendly. *Make a list*, too, of each friendly gesture you've made to each person.

Make these lists regularly. Make them whenever you think people aren't being friendly to you. It doesn't have to be only the people where you work. Use the lists for other people, too.

Activity 9   *Making Friends Checklist*

Why I think they don't like me	Friendly gestures I've made
1. *Office workers—don't ask me to lunch*	*Said hello to some of them one day in elevator*
2. *New neighbors—haven't said hello*	*None*
3.	
4.	
5.	
6.	

Now you have a more true picture of the facts. You can begin to take some risks. Start with things you're sure you can do. You might decide to say good morning to two people at work. Or to give the person at the next desk a compliment.

Build on your success. Try something a little bit harder. For example, you might talk with someone for ten minutes at lunch time. Remember that "success" means doing what you promised yourself to do each day. It has nothing to do with how other people respond to you. You have no control over that.

GETTING TO KNOW PEOPLE IN CLASSES AND ORGANIZATIONS

You spend less time with people in classes and groups than at work. So you'll have to move a little faster to make friends. If you delay, the whole activity might be over before you get started.

How To Begin

A perfect time for informal, friendly talk is before meetings start. Arrange to arrive ten or fifteen minutes early. You'll be one of the first to meet people, to know their names. This will make you feel more secure before the group starts. It will help you to risk being more outgoing.

In a classroom or meeting, look around. Listen. Decide who you're interested in getting to know. Be ready to introduce yourself when there's a break. You might have to walk across the room to do it. For a shy person, it's sometimes hard just to cross a room. But do it anyway.

A few friendly words will start you off. "How long have you been volunteering here?" "Have you taken classes here before?"

Following Up

If all goes well, you'll have a pleasant talk. Be sure to say a word or two again before you leave. "I enjoyed talking with you. See you next week." If you want to be very brave, you might offer the person a ride next week. Or ask her for one.

She may say, "Thanks, but I'm coming from another direction." Don't assume that's a brush-off. She may think it's only a ride you want, not friendship. Don't withdraw into your shell. Make another friendly attempt. If she still doesn't respond, try someone else you think you might like.

Some people you speak to may not have time for a new friend. Don't let that make you feel you're not worth knowing. If you are easily hurt, though, play it safe. Begin by trying to find friends among women who are new in town. Or those who are newly separated from mates and looking for new relationships.

Joan found a good friend in Parents Without Partners. But it was hard at first.

"The first time I went to a Parents Without Partners meeting I was petrified. But I wasn't expected to do anything, and I could just sit there and observe, so I felt safe.... Then I met another woman and we decided to go [to the meetings] together...."

GETTING HELP FROM THE FAMILY

Family members don't always give you support. Maybe you kept your abuse a secret from them before. So it may be hard for them to believe you now. They may blame you for leaving your man. They may need time to get used to the truth.

On the other hand, perhaps family members knew about the abuse all along. They may have urged you to leave, and blamed you when you didn't. Now they expect you to be happy right away. They get impatient with you if you're lonely sometimes. They get angry if you say you're worried about your man. They're afraid you'll go back to him.

Do what you can to explain your feelings to your family. If they go on being negative, protect yourself. Avoid discussions that upset you. Stop seeing family members who make you feel bad. You don't have to make a lot of excuses. You might want to tell them the ways they make you feel bad. But you don't have to. You can just say you feel better when you spend more time alone.

Ask your family to learn about battering. They can read and watch TV programs about it. Check every now and then to see if their ideas have changed. Don't give up on them. They may do things that upset you *because* they care about you. Give yourself time to decide whether they care or not.

Dealing with Kindness

Families who really want to help can also be a problem. They can try too hard to protect you.

For example, maybe you've gone to your parents' house. You just plan to stay for a day or two. But they want you to move in for good. You know it's time to find a place of your own. But it's also comforting and easier to stay with them. So you don't even look at apartment ads.

Such kindness can make you feel helpless. If you see that happening, speak up. Tell your family you need help in becoming independent. That's the best kind of support they can give you.

Chapter 15

The First Week

Your first week on your own may be difficult. Where and how you spend it is important.

STAYING IN A SHELTER FOR BATTERED WOMEN

A battered women's shelter can be helpful. You'll find people there who understand why you left. They'll help you stay away from your partner, if that's what you want. The shelter may have a secret address and phone number. If so, your man won't be able to find you.

Leaving home is hard. You'll be worried about money, childcare, work, or school. Shelter workers will help you sort out your problems. You'll meet other women in situations like yours. Talking with them can make your loneliness and fears easier to handle.

Melissa tried to stay with friends. But her violent boyfriend found out where she was. At last, she went to a battered women's shelter.

"I was frightened when I got there, but they were great, so supportive, and everyone helped everyone and shared stories about how they coped. Everyone had basically the same story.... It still gives me goosebumps to remember the closeness and support I felt then."

Safe Homes

"Safe Homes" are often available in small towns where there are no shelters. There are also Safe Homes in large cities. You will probably be the only guest staying there. A Safe Home is someone's private house. The people who live there give shelter to battered women and their children. It may only be for a few days. But in those few days you will be well cared for. And you will experience life in a nonabusive family.

How to Find a Shelter or Safe Home

First, get information in advance. Don't wait until you're in immediate danger. You can phone this toll-free hot line now: 1-800-333-SAFE. The hot line tells you where the nearest shelter or safe home is.

You can also look in your telephone book for "Battered Women" or "Abused Women." Other listings to look for are:

- a crisis clinic
- a rape crisis line
- the YWCA
- the National Organization for Women
- a college or university Women's Center
- any organization in the book that begins with "Women"

Your small town may have none of these. Try the same listings in the nearest large city or state capital. (Ask your public library for phone books for nearby cities.) You can call a crisis line in another city between 11 p.m. and 8 a.m. Long distance rates are low then.

STAYING WITH FRIENDS OR RELATIVES

It's a comfort to stay with someone who cares about

you. Also, there may be no time-limit on how long you can stay. And with a close friend, you can let out your feelings.

But there are disadvantages, too. It's good for you to let our your feelings sometimes. But it can also encourage you to tell your story over and over. That might be hard for your friend to take. Or it could make her think she should run your life.

It's best to tell your friend or family clearly what you want. And then ask your host to set limits. If you want advice, ask for it. If you want to be let alone, say so. "I might want to hear some advice in a couple of days. But for now, I'd just like to talk about how I feel. Do you mind just listening? And would you tell me when you've had enough?"

Accept help when you really need it. Don't apologize for accepting it. A simple "thank you" is enough. Let your mother babysit while you go to the lawyer or counselor. Borrow your friend's car to look for permanent housing. Just be sure you've both agreed on what's okay. When in doubt, ask.

STAYING ALONE

You may decide to live alone. It could be in a new place. Or it could be in the home you shared with the man.

Perhaps you're fairly sure the man won't come after you. Even so, it's a good idea to change door locks. Put locks on the windows, too. Although it's embarrassing, tell new or old neighbors what's going on. Ask them to call you or the police if they hear sounds of violence. A little embarrassment may mean the difference between life and death.

When you live alone, you have to work hard not to be lonely. Get in touch with friends, relatives, a counselor or a support group. (Review Chapters 13 and 14.) Make a list of crisis line numbers. Keep the list by your telephone. Don't wait until you're desperate to use it.

GROUPS FOR ABUSED WOMEN

It will help you to go to a support group for abused women. Many shelters have these groups. Shelters can also give you information about other support groups in your community.

Joan said it was the women's group that helped her figure things out.

"I was just amazed at the stories of these women and the similarities to mine. I had thought it was all something that I was doing. Peter [my therapist] didn't understand what I was talking about, the feelings, but I could relate to the women, because they had gone through it. I got support and took down a lot of telephone numbers, and... I called. That helped a lot."

CONTACT WITH THE MAN WHO BATTERED YOU

You can give yourself lots of reasons to call the man you left. But wait. Don't do it. Give yourself the same advice you'd give an alcoholic about having just one drink. It's not worth the risk.

For this first week, try to follow two rules. 1. Don't see the man, no matter what. 2. Don't talk to him on the phone, no matter what.

These rules may seem easy the first few days after you've left. You may be able to both see and feel your injuries. You may think you never want to see your abuser again. But sometime during the first or second week, these feelings may change. Your wounds are healing. You may begin to remember happy times with him.

This is an important time. Get ready for it. Here's how.

Most Dangerous List

Make a list of the worst things your partner has done to

you. Include every pain and humiliation. These things are dangerous to your physical and mental health. Include the things he said to you afterward, whether cruel or loving. You're probably going to hear those "loving" promises again. This sheet will help you remember how little they meant. It will help you remember how short the "honeymoon period" was.

Maybe you think you'll never forget the terrible things he's done. But remember the last time you took him back? Didn't you forget then? Write it all down whether you believe you can forget or not. It will be painful. But it could save your life.

Activity 10   Most Dangerous List

_____

_____

_____

_____

_____

_____

_____

_____

_____

_____

Best Memories List

Now make a list of the good things. The happy times, the hopes and dreams. The things you like or admire about the man.

*

Activity 11   **Best Memories List**

_____

_____

_____

_____

_____

_____

_____

_____

_____

_____

Compare the lists. Relive your feelings during good times and bad. Were the good things worth the bad ones?

Change List

"We could be so happy if only he would. . . ." Make a list of the most important "if onlys." What things would he *have* to change for you to risk going back? A sample list might include:

- Never hit me, no matter what I do.
- Not insult me or make fun of me.
- Go to a batterers' group for at least six months.
- Go to AA for at least six months.
- Not try to stop me if I want to see friends, get a job, etc.
- Give me a certain sum of money monthly. No questions to be asked about how I spend it. (We can decide on the amount of money together.)

Activity 12   *Change List*

_____

_____

_____

_____

_____

_____

_____

_____

_____

Check any changes he said he'd make in the past, but didn't. Also *check* those he has refused to discuss with you. Have you any reason to believe things will be different in the future? Has he started to make big changes on any item listed?

If he has started to make some changes, that's good. But wait a while. See how long they last. Is it safe to go back to him because he promised? Or because he says he called a counselor? Or even if he went to a counselor one time?

It's easy for him to promise. The real test is whether he follows through. It will be months before you can be sure.

Using the Lists

Read the lists any time you're tempted to call or see the man. Read the Most Dangerous List aloud. Force yourself to live through the abuse again in your mind. Always keep the list near you. You'll be able to read it any time you feel weak. It can stop you from getting in touch with the man.

Read the Best Memories List, too. You can look at both the good and the bad, and think:

"Yes, Bill can be sweet. He gives me roses. He's fun. He really listens to me sometimes. But those times can never make up for the others. Like the miscarriage he caused, the day he knocked me down the stairs. Or the names he calls me. They make me feel like the lowest person on earth."

Read your Change List. Check the items he's actually changed and for how long a period. Compare what's actually happened with what the list demands. The answer to what you should do will be right there.

Chapter 16

Looking Out for Yourself and the Children

It's harder to leave a man—and stay away—when you have children. This is often true even when the man is not the children's father. This chapter will help you deal with some typical problems.

VISITATION

One of the hardest problems to handle is visits between children and father. You may already be having a hard time keeping away from the man. You may also be feeling guilty about "depriving" the children of their father. His visits with the children will create special risks for you. He'll know how to play on your feelings of guilt and love. The children may also know how to work on your feelings.

You don't have to see him when he sees the children. To avoid seeing him, you'll need to set up their visits carefully. Arrange not to be around when he picks them up. Let him pick them up at a friend, neighbor, or relative's house. Or hire a babysitter, even if you don't like to spend the money. Or arrange for the children to meet him at a child protection agency.

No matter how much trouble it is, avoid seeing him. This is especially important right after you separate.

If you don't have custody, you may be the one visiting the children. You can still avoid seeing him. Use one of the plans just described. Ask your lawyer to write the plans into your divorce decree. Stick to your plans, and insist that he does,too. It's going to be a long time before you can risk seeing this man.

CONTACT WITH THE BATTERER

You may feel friendlier toward your ex-partner after a few months of separation. You might think it's safe to see him now. Maybe just long enough to tell him about Susie's problem with her glasses. You might even think it's safe to have coffee with him. And how much harm could there be in asking him to dinner?

Now is the time to go back to your Change List (Activity 12 in Chapter 15). If you haven't kept the list, ask yourself why. Losing the list may be your way to avoid facing reality.

What Changes Has He Made?

Make a new list that shows the changes he's made. Try hard to remember what was on your first list. Did you decide he needed one year of not drinking? Six months of therapy? Don't reduce those times now. Maybe he's taken a small step in the right direction. You'll still need to wait for some time to see what that means.

You'll also need to ask others whether he's living up to his promises. You may want to see his therapist once (at his expense). He may never even have told the therapist that he batters or drinks. (This often happens.)

Activity 13   What Changes Has He Made?

_____

_____

_____

_____

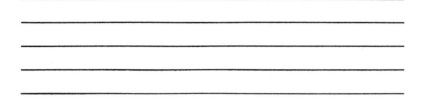

At this point, your ex-partner may play strongly on your guilt feelings. He may accuse you of not trusting him, because you want to check on him. You probably *don't* trust him, after all his empty promises. You have a right to tell him so.

He may insist that he's made a start in the right direction. But he says he has to have your help to continue. You can tell him he'll have to change because *he* wants to. He'll have to change *before* you'll have anything to do with him.

Best of all, *don't* have anything to do with him. You don't have to explain why. "That's just the way I want it." Look away from him and toward a new way of life.

CHILDREN'S REACTIONS TO VIOLENCE AND SEPARATION

After you leave, your children may not see their father at all. A complete break can be good in some ways. The children won't be upset by visits or promises that aren't kept. And neither will you.

On the other hand, the children may long to be with their father. They may blame you for leaving, even if they've seen him beat you. They may want to remember the past as happy. Help them to keep a balanced picture. "Yes, we all miss Daddy. But it's not safe for me to be with him. So this is best."

Some children blame themselves for their parents'

breakup. They may even blame themselves for the violence. If you suspect this, try to get them to talk about it. Listen carefully to the answers. Don't tell a child right away that he or she is wrong. Instead, ask questions that help the child to think clearly. "Would a father leave his child just because she forgot to clean her room? Or because she cried too much?"

Some children will still blame themselves for the man's absence or his violence. Or they may have other problems, like being afraid in a new neighborhood. If so, you might want to get help from a children's counselor.

It's often easier for a child to talk to a counselor than to a parent. Try to find a counselor who works with children of abusers. Most shelters can give you this information.

Nicole's children didn't tell her about their feelings. They never talked about their father, until they saw a counselor:

"My kids started going to counseling and expressing their anger and hatred at Luke. They were mad at me for allowing that man to beat me up and to abuse them and beat them."

⁕When a Child Becomes Violent

Your child may have learned violent behavior from the batterer. This could include hitting, breaking things, bullying by threats or shouts. Make an effort to stop this behavior *every single time* you see it happening. Calmly tell your child that she or he isn't allowed to do that. Gently but firmly take the child to another room. See that the child stays there until he or she regains self-control.

It's important for you to react the same way every time. Never hit the child to "teach him a lesson." Your lesson is that violence is no longer permitted. Don't hit the child if you want to be taken seriously.

Maybe you used to control the child by spanking. So you may slip up sometimes now. Explain to the child that it's a slip-up. You're all trying to learn new ways to treat each other. When you fall back on old ways, that doesn't mean it's right. It just means you have to try harder.

If the violent child is a teenager, you may face hard decisions. A time may come when you think the child threatens the family's well-being. You may even fear for the other children's safety and your own.

You may need to consider drastic action, such as a foster home. It may not have to be for a long period. And sometimes it's the best thing you can do for the child and yourself. It's the strongest way you can say: "No more violence." If this seems your only choice, get some help in making your decision. Call a shelter or child protective services for advice.

When a Child Is "Too Good" or Withdrawn

It's easy to overlook the good child. Good children do just as they're told. They care for the younger children. They comfort you when you're sad. A good child may even begin to act like a parent to you. Maybe you're so sad and tired, you're glad to be taken care of. But remember that children need to be children. They need to know an adult is in charge.

A child may also withdraw, escaping into books, TV, drugs. You don't know what the child is feeling. But the child makes few demands on you. This child, too, is easy to overlook.

It's important to pay attention to children who are "too good" or who withdraw. At some later time, these children may suddenly become angry or destructive. They may have hidden their rage or self-blame for a long time. They need to learn to express their feelings in a positive way. A counselor can sometimes be especially helpful with this.

Don't insist, but do encourage the child to play with other children. Take the child places that will make this easy. Make time to have fun with the child, yourself. Once in a while, you may even need to "baby" the child. She or he may badly need to feel protected, at times.

If you aren't able to do these things yet, find someone who can. A grandparent might help, or a gentle, patient, older baby-sitter.

Whether withdrawn or "too good," your child needs all the support you can offer.

Chapter 17

Teen Abuse

Some teenage women live with the men who abuse them. Some are married, and some have children. If that's your case, most of this book should be helpful. But maybe you're a teenager without children. Perhaps you live with your parents and are battered by your boyfriend. If so, this chapter is especially for you.

Abuse of teenage women by their boyfriends is widespread. Between 25 and 40 percent of teens have been assaulted by dates. About 80 percent of the assaults are pushing, shoving, slaps, and grabbing. But some of the violence is worse. The worst injuries happen when the abuser is drunk.

Teen men are not the only ones hitting. Teenage women hit their boyfriends, too. It can lead to trouble, and sometimes they do serious damage. Especially if they use a weapon.

But teen men are usually able to do more damage than teen women. Most women are not as large or strong as men. So most men are not afraid of women. While women can be emotionally abusive, they rarely control men.

Many teens are raped by dates and boyfriends. Some teen men think it is all right to force sex on women. They think it is all right if the man has spent money on her. Or if she has kissed him. Some teenage women even believe that.

Part of standing up for your rights is knowing that this is *not* all right. It is knowing that forced sex is a form of abuse. Forced sex is rape.

Many adult battered women were teenagers when they started dating the men who batter them. The assaults were often not bad at the beginning. But they got worse as time went on.

May is a Chinese-American who counsels battered Asian women. She was abused, herself, in college and in high school.

"My first boyfriend, when I was thirteen, was very dominating. He studied kung fu and he often liked to spar with me, even though I never knew anything about kung fu. So I had a lot of bruises, but I never thought that he was being abusive to me. ... I remember not wanting sex and yelling at him. It wasn't just talking me into it. It was force, but I never thought of it as rape until I was about twenty-two... [and] seeing a psychologist."

HOW TO TELL IF YOU'RE ABUSED

Sometimes it's hard for a teenager to tell whether she's being abused. Teens often play rough and tease each other. This can sometimes turn into physical or emotional abuse. Here are some examples:

You are playfully wrestling with your boyfriend. He twists your arm behind your back. He's hurting you, but won't let go until you're crying. Or he throws you into a swimming pool "just in fun." Or he takes your purse and shows people private things in it.

You feel embarrassed, scared, or furious. But you laugh, to show you're a good sport. If you don't laugh, your boyfriend says you can't take a joke. You try to make yourself think he's right.

Some teasing is emotional abuse. Maybe yoı boyfriend makes a habit of "jokes" that embarrass you. He may
say insulting things about your body, your friends, or
women in general. Maybe he puts down women as
"broads" or "chicks." Or he calls attention to your large
breasts or your thin legs. The "jokes" and insults become a
pattern. You don't know how to stop it.

Perhaps you tell yourself he doesn't know he's hurting
your feelings. If that's the case, explain it to him. Be serious; tell him without laughing, flirting, or apologizing. He
may say he still doesn't understand. He may say you're too
sensitive or have no sense of humor. Tell him you want
him to stop whether he understands or not.

If he doesn't stop, it's because he doesn't much care
how you feel. He may even tease you purposely to make
you feel bad about yourself. Either way, he's wearing down
your self-esteem. He's abusing you emotionally.

There are many other forms of abuse by teen men.
Some are emotional. Some are physical. Some are a com-
bination of both.

Cars offer some young men a way to show their power.
They may speed or drive recklessly in order to scare their
girlfriends. If you feel scared or helpless, insist that your
boyfriend stop the car. You have a right to get out whenever
you want to.

Your boyfriend may force sex on you. Maybe you've
told him you don't want sex. He says that he will find another girlfriend. Or that if you really loved him, you'd let
him do what he wants. Or that, since you "led him on," he
has a right to intercourse. But that's not true. Your body be-
longs to you.

Maybe you've told your boyfriend to use a rubber. You
want to make sure you don't get V.D. or AIDS. But he
refuses. Or maybe he tells you that you don't need birth

control. He says he'll handle it. He'll pull out in time.

You know that none of these things are safe. But your boyfriend insists. You're afraid to refuse him. You're afraid he might leave you. Or that he will hit you.

WHO'S RESPONSIBLE FOR THE VIOLENCE?

Usually when a man hits a woman, it's more dangerous than when she hits him. Suppose you punch your boyfriend on the arm or pound his chest. He may be three to ten inches taller than you. Maybe he's also thirty to a hundred pounds heavier. He probably won't feel threatened. He might not even try to protect himself.

But if you go on hitting him, some day he might become angry. He might hit you with his fist. That's likely to hurt and scare you. So he might keep doing it, to control you. Then he might blame you, because after all you started it.

If you did start it, you should take responsibility for what you did. Hitting is wrong. But that doesn't mean you're responsible for what *he* did. Only he can start or stop his violence. Only you can start or stop yours.

WHAT TO DO IF YOU'RE HIT

If your boyfriend slaps, pushes, or threatens you, you should take it seriously. Whether or not he's injured you, it's important. It means he's willing to use physical force to control you. It could get worse if you don't put a stop to it. You have to make it absolutely clear you won't allow it.

You must do more than complain. Make sure your boyfriend knows that hitting you is *serious*. That it is *wrong*. And that it is *dangerous*. If he knows, but hits you anyway, then he doesn't care about you.

He may say he cares, but he "couldn't help it." He tells you he won't do it again. He says it's something that "just happened." It was something "out of control."

What if that's really true? Then he can't be sure it won't happen again. So his promises don't mean anything.

He may have been out of control. Or he may have hit you on purpose. Either way, he needs help that you can't give him. He might be helped by a counselor. Or by a kind of group counseling called "anger management." If he says he hit you because he was drunk, he also needs help. He needs alcohol control treatment.

You can insist that he go to counseling or to AA. But if you do, you have to be ready to follow through. You have to risk losing him. Suppose you say, "If you don't go, I'll leave you." And suppose he refuses to go? If you stay with him anyway, that tells him you didn't mean it. He can go on hitting you.

Think clearly about what you really are ready to do. Don't make threats you're not sure you'll carry out. It's better to say something you *know* you can do. "I'm not going to see you for a couple of days." "If you drink when we date, I'll take a bus home."

You can live up to plans like those. And each time you do, you'll feel stronger.

ENDING A RELATIONSHIP

Deciding to break up can be very hard for a teenage woman. It might be especially hard if your relationship was sexual. You may think you can't have another lover for a long, long time. If you do, you're afraid you'll be seen as "loose," or "a slut."

Even if that's not worrying you, you may hesitate. Like many women, you may be afraid you'll never find another man. It's hard to realize that there are other, better men out there. You've been so wrapped up in your abusive boyfriend, you haven't noticed.

It can help a lot to discuss your problems with an understanding person. As a teenager, you may be afraid to confide in anyone. You worry that a doctor, minister, or teacher might tell your parents. They might send your boyfriend away before you've decided what you want. But among people you know, there's probably someone you can talk to safely. It might be a trusted adult or teenage friend. Try talking to your friend now, even if it's painful.

This is the time to talk things over and to think things through. Should you stay in this relationship as a life sentence for a mistake? Or should you give yourself a second chance at a better life? It's the only life you have. There's time left in it for a lot of good things for you.

 *Chapter 18*

Lesbian Abuse

Violence between lesbians has recently come out into the open. Many lesbians have been afraid to say they are abused by their partners. There has not been much support for them from society. Some people are afraid of lesbians and gay men. This fear is called *homophobia.* Because of this fear, it can be hard for battered lesbians to find help.

This situation is starting to change. More and more battered lesbians are speaking out. There are now some services and books for abused lesbians.*

This chapter has some information about lesbian battering. If you're a lesbian who wonders if you are being abused, it may help.

WHO IS BATTERING?

Maybe your partner is the one who hits most often. But sometimes you have hit her in self-defense, or anger. You might think this is "mutual battering." But battering is a *pattern of control.* It is control through both physical and emotional abuse. Your partner may try to make you think you are the batterer. But if you aren't controlling her, you aren't battering. (See the definitions in Chapter 1.)

---

* See *Naming the Violence: Speaking Out About Lesbian Battering,* edited by Kerry Lobel for the National Coalition Against Domestic Violence Lesbian Task Force (Seattle: Seal Press, 1986).

How to Identify Abuse

Sometimes it's hard to tell who is doing the battering. If you are confused, turn to the questions in Chapters 1 and 2. Answer them. Then answer them as your partner would, if she is honest. Does her violence hurt you enough to interfere with work or school? Are you afraid of her? Are you "walking on eggshells"? If you said yes, you are being physically abused.

Are you punished for spending time with friends? For dressing in a way she doesn't like? For going to work or classes she doesn't want you to attend? If you answered yes to any of these, you are being emotionally abused.

If you're being abused in any way, you'll need time away from your partner. If you're being physically abused, your safety is at stake. If you're emotionally or sexually abused, you can be quite confused about it. You'll need time to get to know yourself again. And to like yourself again. And to be with friends who value you.

Suppose you both hit equally often and hard? That means double danger for each of you. You need to get help, whether your partner wants it or not. Suppose, after answering the questions, you think you're the one who batters? If you assault, abuse, or batter your partner, get help. Separate, to get a better look at what you have done. Find a counselor or group to work on your problems.

HOW TO USE *YOU CAN BE FREE*

Most of this book is written for battered women who are not lesbians. However, much of the book can be "translated" for your purposes. You can then apply it to your situation.

You will need to bring special awareness to some parts of the book. This is true, for example, of the advice about police and prosecutors. The way police treat lesbians may be different from the way they treat heterosexuals. Questions about custody differ, too.

You need to bring special awareness to what the book says about self-esteem. (For example, Chapter 11, "You Can Be Your Own Counselor.") You'll need to overcome more than the damage done by your abusive partner. Many people are hostile toward lesbians. That affects the way you feel about yourself, too. You need to guard against accepting hurtful and false views of lesbians.

Ruth was afraid of Robin's violence. But she was also afraid of being known as a lesbian. It was risky for her to be visible.

"Robin would call and say, 'Come back or I'm going to tell your job you're a lesbian' or 'I'm going to tell your family.' The job thing didn't matter much. . . . But my family did matter."

EMERGENCY SERVICES

You're probably hoping you won't ever need emergency services. But if you've thought, even once, that you might, it's best to be prepared. If you're not in a crisis now, this is the time to gather information. Do it while you're calm.

You may have decided that your partner is dangerous. But you've been unwilling to leave her. You might want help from the police at some future time. Check on current police practices and attitudes toward lesbians in your community. Use the information in Chapter 9, but adapt it to your circumstances.

Housing

See Chapter 15 for ways of getting information on emergency housing. For lesbians, choices in almost all cities are limited. In rural towns, there may be "Safe Homes."

However, your hosts might have no sympathy for lesbians. And maybe you'd rather not go into the closet, even temporarily. If you can, make emergency plans for staying with people who will accept you. Talk with your friends about places you might go for safety.

You might want to go to a shelter. You'll need to ask some questions. Is the shelter willing to house lesbians? Some shelters have lesbian and non-lesbian staff who will serve all women equally. But staff attitudes can't guarantee you a welcome from the other women. Some battered lesbians have pretended they were victims of men. But pretending can be hard on you. Here, too, you'll need to decide what's best for you.

ENDING ISOLATION

Refer to the suggestions in Chapters 13 and 14. Also read Chapter 10, on counseling. You can adapt these ideas whether you're in or out of the closet.

If you're out, you'll know which agencies make services available to lesbians. You might not be sure of their attitudes about lesbian battering, however. Phone the agency to ask questions.

Find out whether the agency's program includes help for battered lesbians. Ask about counselors. Are they people who know about battering as well as about lesbian issues? Can they give you information about how police and courts treat battered lesbians?

You might not get satisfactory answers. The agency may not want to deal with issues of lesbian violence. If that's the case, look for programs elsewhere. You can call the National Domestic Violence hot line: 1-800-333-SAFE. The hot line crisis workers understand lesbian battering. Ask them if there is a hot line in your area.

You can also write to the National Coalition Against

Domestic Violence. It has a Lesbian Task Force. The address is: P.O. Box 15127, Washington, D.C. 20003.

Confidentiality

You may not want anyone to know who is battering you. You may not want anybody to know it's happening at all.

Ask about the records an agency keeps. Ask who is allowed to read the files. Don't accept vague answers. Get detailed information from someone who knows how the system works. Where are the files kept? How detailed are they? If you want to read them, how do you get to them?

Perhaps you plan to attend a group or go to counseling. Find out where it will be held. Is it a place where many people will see you come and go? If so, you may run into acquaintances. Are you good at dodging questions like "What brings you here?" If not, look until you find a program in a safer place.

Counseling Services

The agency you like most may have limited services. Perhaps there's no special program for battered women. But there might be a more general support or therapy group. Talk to the leader about discussing battering in her group. Is she open to that? Does she think group members would be accepting? Would she support you no matter what decisions you make?

You can also learn about counseling services by calling shelters and Safe Homes. Crisis lines for battered women offer you crisis counseling. Staff for these agencies might also give you tips on housing, welfare, and police.

In each instance, however, ask staff whether what they're saying applies to lesbians. If they don't always know, they may be willing to find out. This will take some pressure off you. It also adds to their information. This can benefit the next lesbian caller.

Support in the Lesbian Community

Being open about the battering can help you and the whole lesbian community. It's a message to yourself that you're not to blame and not ashamed. To the community it says: "Yes, this is really happening in our own back yard. Isn't it time we did something about it?"

Your first need, of course, is to look out for your own health and safety. So you probably won't risk speaking out unless you expect some support.

Maybe you are afraid to ask a lesbian friend for help. You worry that you will be turned down. Your friend might not believe you are in danger. Or she might be afraid to talk about lesbian battering. So it's good to think carefully about who to ask for help. It's important to find people who believe you.

But you might find more support than you expect. Try speaking to one friend at a time. Start by talking about lesbian battering in general. If your friend seems sympathetic, go on to talk about yourself.

If you're in the closet, you may be afraid to ask for lesbian support. If that's the case, look for a counselor to help you. She should be someone who knows about battering and about lesbian lifestyles. At the very least, she should be willing to learn.

Whatever you decide, you need the help of at least one understanding, caring person. Being battered is hard. Don't make yourself go through the problems alone.

Chapter 19

Toward a New Life

In most chapters of this book, you have seen quotations from women. They come from interviews with many kinds of women. All of the women were battered. All of them got away from their violent partners. You can learn more about them in the book *The Ones Who Got Away*.*

It was not easy for these women to get away. Or to stay away. Or to make a new life. They have had problems in their new lives. They have gone through loneliness. Many of them have had a hard time making ends meet. All of them have been discouraged at times. But they are not sorry they left.

Many other women have been glad that they left abusive partners. Here, in their own words, are some of their reasons.

E.S.: "[I'm] not scared. Before, I could not even say what I want, express what I want. I'm always in fear, before.

"Now I like to go to school. I'm free. Even if I'm poor, I'm happy. I can feel happiness inside now."

Sandi: "Being mostly without a man for almost two years is really lonely sometimes and it's real depressing some-

---

* *The Ones Who Got Away: Women Who Left Abusive Partners,* by Ginny NiCarthy (Seattle: Seal Press, 1987)

times, but I don't think I could have developed into who I am with somebody around. . . . I'm in a space where I really appreciate me. I can believe that I can make decisions on my own. I can raise my kids on my own. . . . It's independence. I can deal with my kids without saying, 'Wait till your father comes home.'"

Valerie: "When he took care of the money, I didn't have that responsibility; I didn't think I wanted it. But now that I've got it, I know a little bit about how good it can feel to have your own and do as you please. I'm going to get along on what money I have and not depend on a man to take care of me."

Patricia: "I'm living with a man who is totally the opposite of what I had before. It's give and take now. I've learned that. I live a normal life now. I have a normal relationship now. . . . I feel like I fit in the world. I'm not being kept in the basement."

Shirley: "I watch TV, I go to see my counselor twice a week, I go to Safeway a lot, you know, maybe to just buy one thing, and I go to the post-office box twice a day. I'm going to be in the phone book in my own name next year, isn't that nice?

"I don't think much past Christmas right now. That's better than it was before, when I didn't think past next week. Things are better for me now because at least there's hope. Before I left Clarence, it was a hopeless situation. It could only get worse."

Marilyn: "The best part of being away is being free, not having anybody criticizing me or telling me what to do. When

I'm out and it's late I don't have to call anybody to make up an excuse about where I am.

"At work I can concentrate, because I'm not in crisis all the time.

"... I'm in the process of probably making major decisions which I've never done. I never made decisions about what I'm going to do with my life. I'm wondering about that now and I'm very slowly looking into possibilities. I'm asking for what I want. I never felt like I could do that."

E.S., Valerie, Sandi, Patricia, Shirley, Marilyn—all have found rewards in life they didn't have before:

"I'm not scared...."
"I can make decisions on my own...."
"I've learned...."
"There's hope...."
"I appreciate myself...."
"I'm free...."

That is their message to you. You, too, can change your life, and you can be free.

Resources

Where to Find Help

National Domestic Violence Hotline
(800) 799-SAFE (7233);
TDD (800) 787-3224

Battered Women's Justice Project
4032 Chicago Avenue South
Minneapolis, MN 55407
(800) 903-0111

Center for the Prevention of Sexual
and Domestic Violence
936 North 34th Street, Suite 200
Seattle, WA 98103
(206) 634-1903

Domestic Abuse Project
204 West Franklin Avenue
Minneapolis, MN 55404
(612) 874-7063

Family Violence Prevention Fund
383 Rhode Island Street, Suite 304
San Francisco, CA 94103-5133
(415) 252-8900

National Coalition Against Domestic
Violence (NCADV)
National Office
P.O. Box 18749
Denver, CO 80218-0749
(303) 839-1852

National Council on Child Abuse
and Family Violence
1155 Connecticut Avenue NW,
Suite 400
Washington, DC 20036
(800) 222-2000
(202) 429-6695

National Victim Center
2111 Wilson Boulevard, Suite 300
Arlington, VA 22201
(800) FYI-CALL
Provides information and referrals,
not crisis counseling.

Seal Press
Orders Department
3131 Western Avenue, Suite 410
Seattle, WA 98121
(206) 283-7844
(800) 754-0271 toll-free order line
Publishes books on domestic
violence.

WOMAN, Inc.
333 Valencia Street, Suite 251
San Francisco, CA 94103
(415) 864-4722
For lesbians in violent relationships.

Women of Color Task Force Against
Domestic Violence
P.O. Box 1743
Aurora, CO 80040
(303) 696-9196

Suggested Reading

The Battered Woman's Survival Guide: Breaking the Cycle by Jan Berliner Statman, Dallas: Taylor Publishing, 1995.

Chain Chain Change: For Black Women in Abusive Relationships by Evelyn C. White, Seattle: Seal Press, 1994.

Defending Our Lives: Getting Away from Domestic Violence and Staying Safe by Susan Murphy-Milano, New York: Anchor Books, 1996.

The Domestic Violence Sourcebook by Dawn Bradley Berry, Los Angeles: Lowell House, 1995.

The Emotionally Abused Woman: Overcoming Destructive Patterns and Reclaiming Yourself by Beverly Engel, New York: Fawcett Columbine, 1990.

Encouragements for the Emotionally Abused Woman: Wisdom and Hope for Women at Any Stage of Emotional Abuse Recovery by Beverly Engel, New York: Fawcett Columbine, 1993.

Getting Free: You Can End Abuse and Take Back Your Life by Ginny NiCarthy, Seattle: Seal Press, 1997.

Healing Your Life: Recovery from Domestic Violence by Candace Hennekens, Pro Writing Services and Press, 1991.

In Love and In Danger: A Teen's Guide to Breaking Free of Abusive Relationships by Barrie Levy, Seattle: Seal Press, 1993.

It's Not Okay Anymore: Your Personal Guide to Ending Abuse, Taking Charge, and Loving Yourself by Greg Enns and Jan Black, Oakland: New Harbinger Publications, 1997.

Mejor Sola Que Mal Acompanada: For the Latina in an Abusive Relationship/ Para la Mujer Golpeada by Myrna M. Zambrano, Seattle: Seal Press, 1985.

Men Who Hate Women and the Women Who Love Them by Dr. Susan Forward, New York: Bantam Books, 1987.

New Beginnings: A Creative Writing Guide for Women Who Have Left Abusive Partners by Sharon Doane, Seattle: Seal Press, 1996.

Recovery of Your Self-Esteem: A Guide for Women by Carolyn Hillman, New York: Fireside/Simon & Schuster, 1992.

Violent Betrayal: Partner Abuse in Lesbian Relationships by Claire Renzetti, Newbury Park, CA: Sage Publications, 1992.

What's a Nice Girl Like You Doing in a Relationship Like This? Women in Abusive Relationships edited by Kay Marie Porterfield, Freedom, CA: The Crossing Press, 1992.

When "I Love You" Turns Violent by Scott A. Johnson, Far Hills, NJ: New Horizon Press, 1993.

When Love Goes Wrong: What to Do When You Can't Do Anything Right by Ann Jones and Susan Schechter, New York: HarperPerennial, 1992.

About the Authors

Ginny NiCarthy's name is familiar to tens of thousands of women as the author of *Getting Free: You Can End Abuse and Take Back Your Life*, the groundbreaking book on abuse of women by intimate partners that has now sold over 150,000 copies. Ms. NiCarthy is also the co-author of three other important books: *Talking It Out: A Guide to Groups for Abused Women*, *The Ones Who Got Away: Women Who Left Abusive Partners* and *You Don't Have to Take It!: A Woman's Guide to Confronting Emotional Abuse at Work* (all published by Seal Press). Ginny NiCarthy has been active in the movement to end violence against women for over 20 years as a writer and counselor. She has been instrumental in starting programs for rape victims and battered women, including groups for lesbians and women of color. She lives in Seattle.

Sue Davidson is a freelance writer and editor who has worked with the advocacy organization New Directions for Young Women. She edited and contributed to *The Second Mile: Contemporary 0Approaches in Counseling Young Women*. She is the author of the *Women Who Dared* series, multicultural biographies of pioneering American women written for adults learning to read and young adults. The first two volumes profile journalists and politicians: *Getting the Real Story: Nellie Bly and Ida B. Wells* and *A Heart in Politics: Jeanette Rankin and Patsy T. Mink*. The most recent volume profiles tennis players Alice Marble and Althea Gibson and is titled *Changing the Game*.